Rants from the Bunker

Rants from the Bunker

Facebook posts and Debates

In the Obama Era

BY

DR. TIM KIRBY

Dedicated

To

Mom

For encouraging me to be

an independent thinker

I miss you

"Neither current events nor history show that the majority rule, or ever did rule." – Jefferson Davis

Forward

The Reverend Dr. Timothy D. Kirby and I grew up within 3 miles of each other, have similar religious and class backgrounds, and are separated by about 4 years of age. Neither of our sets of parents were divorced, we attended the same elementary and high schools, and have/had many of the same friends. With so many similarities in our formative years, it should be no surprise that we share similar attitudes and sensibilities about a great many things. This is certainly true in the broadest terms but what this has to do with you, gentle reader, is this: while Dr. Kirby and I are in agreement on most topics politically, he always manages to come up with an angle that I didn't expect. A born storyteller, a natural contrarian, his opinions, monologs, sermons, rants and diatribes are always entertaining, generally informative, and sometimes even mind bending. I am pretty sure that I agree with whatever is in the book but at this point I haven't the slightest idea what that is. So buckle up, we are about to find out.

Andrew Hoag

Acknowledgments

There are several people who, without them, this would not have been possible. I want to single out just a couple of my debate opponents for thanks. First and foremost, Jammin' Jimmy Bean. A truly great liberal, sorry Jim, progressive, and a hell of a great guy. And folks like Tina Gooch, Bill Gorrell, Michael Tipsword, and Robin Randolph; all worthy opponents.

Also, Lisa Hoag, for being a "real mixer". Never before since Eve, has one woman stirred up so much trouble. And Drew Hoag, my sounding board, and the one person who has to listen to me rant face to face.. And all of my conservative friends who sided with me in these debates.

And a special thanks to Terri Heath for suggesting the basis for the title. And to Anthony Cumia for inspiration.

Lastly, my family. My father for putting up with me for 43 years. And my sons, Tyler and Dean, for never vocally questioning my sanity.

Preface

I got the idea to do this book from all of my Facebook friends. I have received so many positive comments from my friends about my status updates and posts, even from people who vehemently disagree with me, that I thought I should look into putting them together in book form. My main reason for doing this is so that my children will have this to remember me by when I am gone. And so that my grandchildren will be able to get some idea of what "Grandpa" was all about.

Compiling all of these posts was a labor of love. It was fun to go back through the last year and see the different debates that I had been a part of that I did not even remember.

I stuck strictly with the political posts for this book. Perhaps sometime I will go back through and compile all of my posts, but for now I think this is the way to go. We are at a turning point in our growth as a nation where we are either going to uphold our core values of we are going to go in a radical new direction. Whatever happens, I am glad that I was here to see it. We are truly living as history is unfolding around us.

When I was putting this together I tried to maintain as much of the original flavor of the postings as possible. I did correct spelling and punctuation in my posts as well as those of others simply to make them easier to read. I left any colloquialisms and as much of the grammar as I could intact so that the personality of the poster could come through in their words. I also went back and cited sources for some of my posts that did not get cited in their original form. There were some posts that I edited out of debates because they were extremely off topic or in some cases crude, but nothing that would take away from the debate by being missing. Finally, I changed all of my posts to **bold and italic** text for ease of differentiating the posters.

This book is set in a pretty straight forward fashion. First the threads from my Facebook page. Then some posts that stood on their own. Then the chapters that were the most fun; A debate from Tina Gooch's page, Wesley Cramer's page and Lisa Hoag's page. Then the last half of the book is a series of very spirited exchanges from Jammin' Jimmy Bean's page between me, Jim, and his left leaning friends. With just a few of his more conservative friends helping me out. And finally, a response to an essay by Rosie O'Donnell.

Appendix 1 is my treatise on religion that originally appeared in a thread on Health Care reform.

I hope you enjoy reading these pages as much as I enjoyed ranting the words on them.

Threads from My Page

October 9, 2009 – Obama's Nobel Prize

Tim Kirby - *Obama wins Nobel Peace Prize after less than 1 year in office and while presiding over 2 wars?!?!? WTF??*
October 9, 2009 at 10:51am

Jeff Miller - And I personally don't see ONE thing that he has done except Whore himself out and write checks that we can't cash
October 9, 2009 at 10:55am

Jeff Miller - He is just like the kid on South Park....TOKEN...so that white America can feel better about what their ancestors did
October 9, 2009 at 10:59am

Tina Gooch - Actually, he was nominated for the Noble Peace Prize 2 weeks prior to winning the Presidential Election so it was not anything he has done since being in office.
October 9, 2009 at 11:18am

Tim Kirby – *That's even worse. He didn't do ANYTHING before he was elected*
October 9, 2009 at 11:31am

Tina Gooch - Apparently he did according to these quotes. The Nobel Committee said it decided to honor Obama for his "extraordinary efforts to strengthen international diplomacy and cooperation between peoples." "Only very rarely has a person to the same extent as Obama captured the world's attention and given its people hope for a better future," the committee said.

2

Jagland said the decision was "unanimous" and came with ease.

October 9, 2009 at 11:47am

Tina Gooch - Sorry Tim.... as you can tell I am a huge Democrat and can't let negative comments get by me....LOL...

October 9, 2009 at 11:47am

Tim Kirby - *I wasn't really looking at it as a Democrat/Republican thing. I was more looking at the body of work. I totally understood when Jimmy Carter got his. Not a great president but does a lot of good with Habitat for Humanity. And a couple of years ago I was against Limbaugh's nomination. I like him but he hasn't done anything to earn a peace prize. You have to admit Obama is pretty young and hasn't really done anything to earn it. Basically he got it because he is not George Bush. The head of the committee said as much. Maybe in time he will do something to earn it but giving it now is like giving an Academy Award to someone who may be going to make a great movie next year. Also, if you give the peace prize too early you set up an embarrassing situation like 1939 when the prize was given to Hitler and had to be taken away later. Don't forget that we are sending more troops to Afghanistan and are thinking about bombing Iran. Both need done but neither is very peaceful*

October 9, 2009 at 12:08pm

Lisa Hoag - All I want 2 say is.....I didn't vote for this Obamanation!

October 9, 2009 at 12:18pm

3

Tim Kirby - *That's all well and good Lisa, but as I said, this isn't really a political thread and doesn't have anything to do with party affiliation or who voted for whom.*
October 9, 2009 at 12:26pm

Lisa Hoag - Still.....I didn't vote for this Obamanation. That's all I have to say WHENEVER his name is mentioned. Political discussion or not......I'm not trying to keep the peace LOL!
October 9, 2009 at 12:31pm

Kelly Reese - Lisa you didn't vote for him...but did u vote?
October 9, 2009 at 12:51pm

Jeff Miller - I just think if his skin was white and his name was Bob, he wouldn't get a damn thing. Sorry
October 9, 2009 at 12:51pm

Jeff Miller - Prior to him running in the Election, virtually nobody ever heard of the guy
October 9, 2009 at 12:53pm

Lisa Hoag - Hell YES I voted!!!!
October 9, 2009 at 12:59pm

Tim Kirby - *Voting Republican in Illinois is the same as not voting.*
October 9, 2009 at 1:05pm

Lisa Hoag - LOL that's about right!
October 9, 2009 at 1:08pm

Kelly Reese - But ya gotta vote...that's just American!!! I did

too Lisa...and not for the man in office.
October 9, 2009 at 2:07pm

January 28, 2010 - Obama

Tim Kirby - *Is there anyone left who can HONESTLY say that they believe Obama is qualified to be president? Even those on the left are seeing it now.*
January 28 at 2:02pm

Carrie Williams Orwig - I would have Obama any day before I would have Sarah Palin anywhere near the white house. Sorry but that woman scares the hell out of me
January 28 at 2:08pm

Tiffany Atkinson - And that is what America gets for putting someone in office with no experience....
January 28 at 2:08pm

Lisa Hoag - No worries about Sara Palin now, just grateful the great hope is now being seen for the mac daddy he is!!! LOL!!
January 28 at 2:12pm

Tiffany Atkinson - I think everyone thought he was going to do great things for this country but, instead has done more damage in a year than any President so far...he needs booted out!!
January 28 at 2:13pm

Carrie Williams Orwig - I am not happy at all with Obama...he has made things worse but he is also trying to mop up GW's 8 year mess also
January 28 at 2:15pm

Lisa Hoag - He has missed a few spots! =}
January 28 at 2:16pm

Shawn Cunningham - I don't think anyone, short of maybe Lincoln, could clean up the mess the country has turned into. They especially couldn't do it in only a year. I think people are jumping the gun a little with so much criticism so prematurely. Much of the problems, especially the economic downfall, is a result of decades of Republican control. Much of which had a great amount of short-term success, but had very negative long-term consequences. So it's very naive to think that all of these problems should have been fixed by now. Granted, he did promise more results than he has produced, so far.
January 28 at 3:55pm

Tiffany Atkinson - Ok Shawn you put years of Republican control but, Bush was only in office for 8 years and Clinton for 8 which was a Dem. Clinton is actually the one to change the housing rules we have today which made the mess...I agree everyone is allowed their opinion but, Obama is and will do more harm to this country in 4 years then bush did in 8 or any other president before him. He has spent more money in a year then bush did in 8.
We can't accept a President who refuses to take blame when after a year in office still points the finger at Bush
January 28 at 4:06pm

6

Lisa Hoag - Go Tiffany!!!!
January 28 at 4:25pm

Tim Kirby - *Well said Tiffany. Shawn, that was spoken like a true college student. ;-) What I was getting at was that a community organizer with 2 years of experience in the Senate is not qualified to lead the country. Add to that his extreme socialist agenda and you see that he is completely out of touch with what America is all about. If you listened to his speech last night what you heard was a megalomaniacal individual who is in need of serious therapy. It is time to let go of the ghost of Bush and take responsibility. He spent more money in one year than Bush did in the last four. He also needs to stay out of the public sector. Nationalizing the banks, health care, and the auto industry is the stuff of banana republics and dictators like Chavez.*
January 28 at 4:28pm

Tim Kirby - *For the record, I don't think Lincoln was that great either, even if he was a republican. He started an illegal war in violation of the articles of confederation. The south was totally within its rights to leave, and no, it was not about freeing slaves. Slavery was on its way out anyway, and the only slaves Lincoln freed were southern, no northern slaves were freed. We are still dealing with the fallout of that war today.*
January 28 at 4:34pm

Shawn Cunningham - Actually, I agree with both of you. I don't believe Obama has been even remotely good as a

president. I think he won on hype alone and definitely does not have the experience to be in the position he is in, especially given the current state of the nation. I was just saying that many people are jumping the gun on so much criticism, so early in his term. Most times the first half of a president's term is spent dealing with and tying up the loose ends left by his predecessor. Bush was unique because of 9/11. Also, the biggest factor in the economic downturn was the housing market, but it was caused by the laws enacted under Clinton. They were a result of the dirty and unfair practices of Wall Street distributing riskier and riskier loans for the last 40 or so years. (The majority of which was ran by Republican presidents.)
January 28 at 4:40pm

Shawn Cunningham - In Lincoln's time Republicans and Democrats were almost completely different than they are today. So, him being a Republican is actually irrelevant. I also think that the Civil War was fought, not over slavery, but of State's individual rights. Whether you think the war was right or wrong, it was still a good thing for the country. Had the nation been permanently divided, do you think that the US would be the prominent power it is today? It's very doubtful. The World Wars would definitely have been different. We would probably be under Nazi control right now.
January 28 at 4:47pm

Tiffany Atkinson - very true Shawn the thing is our country was not founded by either Rep. or Dem. but our first president was a Federalist and the reason our country split to Dem and Rep. is because his Sec. of State Jefferson and Sec. of Treasury Hamilton couldn't agree which is how the two founded. So looking back on the start of our country it was never founded by Rep. or Dem. but just by the choice of freedom. Which I think our country needs to get back to. We have way too much Gov. in our lives as it is. They keep taking from the middle class and giving to the rich (in tax breaks) or giving the poor (welfare programs) and that is why our country is going broke.

We as American's need to stand up and say enough is enough and I think that is small areas it is happening. Sorry to get all political this is a sour subject for me
January 28 at 4:58pm

Tim Kirby - *Don't be sorry tiffany. My original post was meant to be provocative and get people debating and that is what it did.*
January 28 at 5:21pm

Tiffany Atkinson - Ok Tim what are you an English Teacher...that is what all my high school and College English teacher do....
January 28 at 6:30pm

Wesley Cramer - Well, I think Lincoln planted the seeds of the progressive movement at the turn of the century. He was a well-spoken, intellectual man that, while I highly respect, I also think he was often wrong. He himself openly admitted exceeding constitutional authority on purpose. He was a tax and spender. If states came into the Union on their own accord, why could they not leave on their own accord - after all, the Union was analogous to a club that states could join and the only clubs I know of that won't let you quit after you join are usually called gangs.....

Obama vs. Palin... well, Obama thinks the constitution is a flawed document - his words - Palin thinks it is a document from which governance should be based - point to Palin. Both live their political beliefs - point to Palin. Based upon basic core belief systems, I'd trust a quirky and suspect Palin to the ostensibly erudite Obama who frankly does not hold American principles embodied in the constitution - it is scary to think he's an alleged scholar thereof.

January 28 at 8:33pm

Darla McFarland Sigmon - Tim thanks for the great discussion. I agree with both you and Wesley. I agree Lincoln was an early progressive. He started the Federal Income tax. Then along came Teddy Roosevelt and FDR who were both huge progressives and laid the ground work for today's mess.

January 29 at 7:45am

Wesley Cramer - YEAH! I was a bit concern y'all would think I was off my rocker on the Lincoln observation... I still like the guy though.

January 29 at 5:01pm

March 19, 2010 – The Slaughter Solution

Tim Kirby - *Obama has stated that if "Slaughter" works with health care, he will not rule out using it on other* *pieces of his agenda. Apparently, not having majority support from congress is not going to be a deterrent in his quest to end capitalism and 250 years of the American way of life. Welcome to the dictatorship. We are officially a banana republic. The sad thing to me is that there a people celebrating this.*

March 19 at 11:16pm

Doug Maddox - What is "slaughter"?
March 19 at 11:42pm

Tim Kirby - *The "Slaughter Solution" was conceived by Rep. Louise M. Slaughter, D-New York as a way to pass the bill without a vote. The House will deem that the Senate bill passed and then they will use reconciliation to add amendments later. It is way to for Dems on the fence to let it pass and still be able to tell their constituents that they did not vote for it. It is also referred to a "Deem and Pass" or "Demon Pass" if you prefer. It is in total violation of Article 1, Section 7 of the Constitution which states that for any bill to become a law, it must "pass both the House of Representatives and the Senate. That is, not be "deemed" to have passed, but actually be voted on with the support of the required majority. The bill must contain the exact same language in both chambers - and in the version signed by the president - to be a legitimate law. This is why the House and Senate have a conference committee to iron out differences of competing versions. This is Civics 101."*

"It is a dagger aimed at the heart of our system of checks and balances. It would enable the Democrats to establish an ominous precedent: The lawmaking process

11

can be rigged to ensure the passage of any legislation
without democratic accountability or even a congressional
majority."[1]

It's the road to tyranny. IMHO
March 19 at 11:53pm

Tim Kirby - *FYI, if they go through with it, it could be*
deemed an impeachable offense by the House leadership
and the President if he signs it. There are already 3 states
drafting law suits against the Federal Government if it
passes and I think Texas and Alaska might even try to
secede. They have been talking about it for a while now.
March 19 at 11:56pm

Doug Maddox - Incredible. I would never, even one year
ago, have thought that our country would come to this. I
really didn't like Bill Clinton, but he at least cared somewhat
what the people thought...Obama has no care for the
people...even the people who voted for him. He used them
to get into office, but doesn't have any real use for them.
March 20 at 12:49am

Doug Maddox - And, btw, thanks for clearing that up,
Tim...hadn't heard of that before...guess I've been under a
rock, or something...
March 20 at 12:50am

Tim Donaldson - What is most amazing about this, is that
those who were the Anti-Establishment, are now the

---

[1] Jeffrey T. Kuhner, "Impeach the President," Washington Times,
March 19, 2010

Establishment, and doing worse things to our Democratic Republic than all of the things they protested combined! But at least it's all for "THE GREATER GOOD"!!!!!!!
March 20 at 12:49pm

March 19, 2010 – Niemoller Adaptation

Tim Kirby - *I would like to paraphrase Pastor Martin Niemöller, and no disrespect intended in changing this classic holocaust poem. I just think it works as well today.*
March 19 at 11:31pm

Tim Kirby - *THEY CAME FIRST for the gun owners,*

and I didn't speak up because I wasn't a gun owner.

THEN THEY CAME for the banks,

and I didn't speak up because I wasn't a banker.

THEN THEY CAME for the Auto Industry,

and I didn't speak up because I wasn't an Auto worker.

THEN THEY CAME for the Churches,

and I didn't speak up because I wasn't a church goer.

THEN THEY CAME for me

and by that time no one was left to speak up.
March 19 at 11:31pm

Kevin Cunningham - i worked for a lady a while back her and her husband come from wealthy families she said to me there is no recession people are just using that as a crutch. Was she insane is she so rich that it don't affect her is she living in a box i just wanted to slap her
March 20 at 5:31am

Kevin Cunningham -speaking of this wonderful economy here's some advice if you have more than 100 dollars invested anywhere get it out and bury it before they take.19 years I've contributed to my retirement fund and their taking it no vote no voice just taking it.
March 20 at 5:33am

Penny Hanson - really thinks you should run for some office.....I would vote!
March 20 at 7:47am

Tiffany Atkinson - Tim have you ever watch Beck...I think you would like him.....u guys talk about all the same topics
March 20 at 10:52am

Tim Kirby - *@Tiff, I am not a big fan of Glen Beck. We have similar views but he is a little bit too out there for me in the way he presents them.*

@Penny I ran for local office several years ago without much luck. I can't run for anything higher than that because they would unseal my divorce records and (based on Jack Ryan) I would be forced to withdraw anyway, with people KNOWING I'm nuts instead of just thinking it. Besides, your mom would come back to haunt you if you

voted for a Republican (I miss your mom). But thanks for the kind words

@Kevin, A good friend of mine actually did cash in all his retirement and savings and bought gold. Not, the stock certificates that say you own gold, but the physical gold. I wouldn't be surprised if he had it buried somewhere.
March 20 at 12:15pm

March 19, 2010 Star Wars Quote

Tim Kirby - *"So this is how liberty dies...with thunderous applause." - Padme Amidala*
March 19 at 11:16pm

Kelly Reese - With sadness in the hearts of many....
March 19 at 11:17pm

March 23, 2010 – Ronald Reagan

Tim Kirby - *"Freedom is never more than one generation away from extinction. We didn't pass it to our children in the bloodstream. It must be fought for, protected, and handed on for them to do the same, or one day we will spend our sunset years telling our children and our children's children what it was once like in the United*

States where men were free." - Ronald Reagan
March 23 at 12:02am

Wesley Cramer - Amen. I have an RR calendar on the wall. He speaks of eternal optimism and that he believes, even after his passing in one quote, that America's best days are ahead. He must be wondering now. Our founders must be shedding tears of blood by now.
March 23 at 3:19am

Tara Huchel-nestich - Wonder what he would say if he were here today?
March 23 at 5:10am

Darla McFarland Sigmon - Ronald Reagan was such a wise man. I so wish he were here today, to help us straighten out this mess. I am sad for my children and their future.
March 23 at 7:41am

Doug Maddox - amazing that Obama tried so hard to make us think he was like Lincoln, but everything he does is contradictory to what Lincoln would do...
March 23 at 3:20pm

Tim Kirby - *I don't know Doug, like I said in a previous post Lincoln divided the country too. And he ignored the constitution, and overstepped his authority. So maybe not so different? I read a great book once that hypothesized that had Lincoln not bill killed he would have become a Marxist.*
March 23 at 3:46pm

Doug Maddox - Wow, Tim, hadn't heard that one...thought all of his actions were to bring the country that was already divided back together...I see how you might say that

because of his hard stand on national over states' rights caused some to secede, but, I always felt like he wanted to bring the nation back together...interesting perspective.
March 23 at 3:51pm

Tim Kirby - *Lincoln chose to exert his will onto the people by force. It was he that ordered the first shots on Ft. Sumter. The articles of confederation gave any state the right to leave the Union, which they had entered voluntarily. Lincoln completely ignored this fact when he chose war. He also stripped the people of fundamental rights when he suspended habeas corpus.*
March 23 at 4:23pm

Tim Kirby - *In 1990-91 when the Baltic states were seceding from the Soviet Union we were the first to step up and defend their right to do so. It is my belief that the next decade or so TX and AK will both vote to secede and we will see how far we have come. Also, a drive through AL or MS even today will show that the scars from Lincoln's misguided war and Andrew Johnson's botched reconstruction still have not healed.*
March 23 at 4:34pm

Tim Kirby - *Jeez, how did I go from attacking our Marxist president to a dissertation on the Civil War? Sorry to bore all my FB friends. In the future I will try to stay on point.*
March 23 at 4:37pm

Darla McFarland Sigmon - Your words are true, and I have enjoyed reading them. I agree that TX and AK will probably leave the union at some point. My daughter was born in

17

Texas, and we lived there for 5 years. I understand Texans, and I don't blame them.
March 23 at 4:42pm

Wesley Cramer - If Texas goes, I think I will be with them....
March 23 at 8:29pm

March 23, 2010 – Facebook Page Down

Tim Kirby - *It seems a little strange to me that after my anti-Obama, anti-left rant last night, for several hours I was unable to access my FB page. Any time I tried to log in I got a message that my page was unavailable due to maintenance. It wasn't all of FB though because I was able to sign into Russell's page and could view all of my friend's pages through Russell. Coincidence or is big brother watching and censoring?*
March 23 at 12:16pm

Robert W. Ford - Well if the shoe fits...
March 23 at 4:27pm

Jammin' Jimmy Bean - Just because you're paranoid doesn't mean they're not out to get you. (^:
March 23 at 10:04pm

March 23, 2010 – Tanning Tax

Tim Kirby - *The first new tax of the health care bill went into effect today. Tanning salons now have to charge a 10% tax for tanning. I guess only people who make over $200000/yr. tan because I was told they were the only ones to be taxed. Also, this tax unfairly directed at only the pale percentage of the population???*
March 23 at 9:09pm

Jammin' Jimmy Bean - Quite a stretch tonight Tim, don't you think? It's a luxury tax.
March 23 at 9:12pm

Tim Kirby - *I'm just sayin' we have been told that the only people who would see ANY new taxes would be those making over 200k. Luxury or not it IS a new tax.*
March 23 at 9:23pm

Pamela Holler Flaningam - I sure don't make that much! I guess I will have to tan the free way. Well, if it's ever warm & sunny again that is!
March 23 at 9:42pm

March 23, 2010 - Stupak

Tim Kirby - *And now we know the truth about Stupak! "Obama Administration Awarded Hundreds of Thousands in Airport Grants to Stupak's District Two Days Before*

Vote" I guess his pro-life position WAS for sale.
March 23 at 9:16pm

Tim Kirby - *And, he still has the nerve to say that Rep. Randy Neugebauer's 2 apologies for his "baby killer" comment on the House floor are not enough and he needs to apologize during a House session. Seems to me if you are going to sell out something you say you believe in, and then take whatever comes at you. It would be different if he had taken a pro-choice stance all along.*
March 23 at 9:21pm

Doug Maddox - Neugerbauer is just telling the truth. No apology needed.
March 23 at 9:24pm

March 23. 2010 – Secret Police

Tim Kirby - *I am going to bed. I can't stay up all night trashing the administration again. Besides, I think the Secret Service, the FBI and Homeland Security are all monitoring my FB page now.* До свидания товарищ.
March 23 at 10:40pm

Tim Kirby - *I wanna see one of y'all translate that one!*
March 23 at 10:40pm

Jammin' Jimmy Bean - If they ARE checking you out you can thank G Dub for the Homeland Security Act. (^: (Sleep tight!)
March 23 at 10:43pm

March 24, 2010 – Health Care Reform

Tim Kirby - *I want to make the Health Care debacle clearer for my less politically savvy friends. This is too long for a status so be sure to read the comment*
March 24 at 9:39am

Tim Kirby - *Think of it like a marathon race with everyone striving for the finish line. You train really hard and are able to lead the race from start to finish through your hard work. Now, say there are some others in the race who did not train at all and are not able to keep up with you and the others out front. So, it is decided that you have to run the race wearing a bomb disposal suit and weights. But that's not all; you also have to use money out of your pocket to buy motorcycles for the people in the back to ride so they can do better.[2] That is the health care bill (and socialism) in a nut shell. Hope the clarifies for everyone who couldn't understand why everyone else was so upset.*
March 24 at 9:45am

Tiffany Atkinson - Nice way of putting it Tim...now if they don't understand we'll just say they aren't the brightest light bulb
March 24 at 1:07pm

---

[2] Anthony Cumia, The Opie and Anthony Show, 2010

21

March 23, 2010 – Night Off

Tim Kirby - *Hey gang, I am going to take a night off from my political soapbox. I didn't want y'all thinking I wasn't posting because the Secret Police kicked in my door. I am just too tired to be enlightening, educational and funny tonight. I am just going to spend the evening locked in my bunker watching Survivor and tweeting with some of the former contestants.* До свидания товарищ.
March 24 at 5:40pm

Tim Kirby - *Still waiting for someone to translate that last sentence. :-)*
March 24 at 5:41pm

Missy Miller - Not from me!!
March 24 at 5:44pm

Angie Ruwe - me too! How long are you gonna make us wait?
March 24 at 11:11pm

March 24, 2010 – Shots Fired

Tim Kirby - *I thought the leftists won. Why are they still being violent? Some leftist fired shots through the window of the minority whips office. SAVAGES!*
March 25 at 1:25pm

Missy Miller - Because that's just how they are Tim...Idiots!!!
March 25 at 1:28pm

Tim Kirby - *I am afraid these are only the first shots of the 2nd American Civil War.*
March 25 at 1:29pm

March 24, 2010 – Buck's Place

Tim Kirby - *Hey Gang, Head over to my new Cafe Press store and pick up your very own "Obama is a douche" and "Communism, not the change we were expecting" t-shirts. More designs to come soon.*

Buck's Place

Cafepress.com/bucknekkid
March 25 at 5:26pm

Jammin' Jimmy Bean -I'm certain that this will make things better.
March 25 at 5:39pm

Tim Kirby - *It makes me smile. If it makes you feel better though, the $1.00 I make on each shirt is taxed. LOL*
March 25 at 5:40pm

Tim Kirby - *I just added a selection of "Teabagger, Say NO to taxes" golf shirts, polo shirts, and underwear. Also*

added bumper stickers of all three slogans.
March 25 at 6:20pm

Tim Kirby - *Almost forgot, I also added a Teabagger button.*
March 25 at 6:22pm

Missy Miller - You are cracking me up....Keep it up.
March 25 at 6:58pm

Tim Kirby - *Be sure and buy a shirt or button Missy. That is a real store that I opened.*
March 25 at 7:25pm ·

Missy Miller - Shirt or Button? Why can't I get the underwear?
March 25 at 8:21pm

Missy Miller - I'll buy the Say NO to taxes and wear it to work. Think that would be ok?
March 25 at 8:22pm ·

Tim Kirby - *You can get underwear if you want. I got boxers, boy shorts and thongs.*
March 25 at 9:02pm

Missy Miller - Ha-ha ok Tim. I think I will take the boxers. ha-ha
March 25 at 9:58pm

Israel

Tim Kirby - *I am embarrassed for the country.*
March 25 at 7:09pm

Tim Kirby - *While Binyamin Netanyahu was at the White House for talks, which as we have all heard by now did not go well, our disgrace of a President actually left him sitting in the Roosevelt room and went to dinner. Obama told Mr. Netanyahu to consult with his advisors and "let me know if there is anything new." I cannot believe we are treating one of our strongest allies this way. At least Israel used to be our strongest ally. It is disgraceful to humiliate Mr. Netanyahu like that. What makes it even worse is that this is the same President who BOWED to the King of Saudi Arabia! And he is taking a more relaxed stand on Iran and not pursuing sanctions over their nuclear ambitions. Yea, sure he converted from Islam. I think it is sad that Israel, who is surrounded by enemies, is now going to have to go it alone because we managed to elect a president with more sympathy towards the Muslim dictators and monarchs of the area, than of the only Western style democracy in the Middle East. It is an embarrassment.*
March 25 at 7:16pm

Doug Maddox - We only have what we have because we are an Allie of Israel. Without that our country is doomed.
March 25 at 8:28pm

March 24, 2010 – Podcast?

Tim Kirby - *What do y'all think, should I start a podcast? Live from the bunker.*
March 25 at 9:05pm

Kim S Coon – yep
March 25 at 9:08pm

Jeff Miller - Yes. You need to have an Assault rifle on you at all times and some War paint on your face.
March 25 at 9:10pm

Tim Kirby - *Trust me Jeff, I am armed.*
March 25 at 9:15pm

Jeff Miller - I'm talking about for the WebCam so your viewers can see you ready to kick ass
March 25 at 9:18pm

Bob Brown - watch out for the black helicopters!!
March 25 at 9:18pm •

Tim Kirby - *I was really thinking more of an audio kind of thing. It has been said that I have the perfect looks for radio.*
March 25at 11:34pm

Darla McFarland Sigmon - Yes!
March 26 at 7:43am

March 25, 2010 – Learn Russian

Tim Kirby - До свидания товарищ.
March 25 at 11:41pm

Jammin' Jimmy Bean - That's exactly what I was thinking. (^:
March 25 at 11:48pm

March 25, 2010 – Learn Arabic

Tim Kirby - *I think I will switch it up a little tonight. I know I already did my Russian closer for the day, but I would like to redo it in Arabic since our government is throwing Israel under the bus so to speak.* أصــــدقائي يـا الخــير مساء
March 25 at 11:53pm

Tim Kirby - *And in Hebrew because I DO support Israel.* **Lella tov chaverim.**
March 25 at 11:54pm

March 26, 2010 – Korean Ship Sinking

Tim Kirby - *South Korean Navy vessel sinking in the Yellow Sea after a suspected torpedo attack by the North. 100 sailors on board.*
March 26 at 10:39am

Tim Kirby - *Now we will see if General Secretary Obama is willing to take a hard stance against one of his Communist buddies in favor of one of our longtime allies.*
March 26 at 10:43am

March 26, 2010 – Ready Reserve Corps

Tim Kirby - *Well, he did it. During the campaign Obama called for a civilian security force equal to the military.*
March 26 at 1:06pm

Jammin' Jimmy Bean - It's a beautiful day today. Have a Coke and a smile.
March 26 at 1:09pm

Tim Kirby - *The HC bill creates a Ready Reserve Corps to be activated during "national emergencies. These people will be appointed by the president without confirmation by Congress. You all thought I've been joking about the secret police.*
March 26 at 1:11pm

Jammin' Jimmy Bean - O.K. then, I'll have one and smile for you.
March 26 at 1:16pm

Greg Peace - Tim we already have Homeland Security. I was under the impression that was the same thing.
March 26 at 1:29pm

Tim Kirby - *This is Obama's personal security force. Hand-picked by him with no oversight.*

March 26 at 1:37pm

Michael Tipsword - 42 U.S.C. 204 It states ""involuntary calls to active duty during national emergencies and public health crises and it appears:

(3) APPOINTMENT.—Commissioned officers of the Ready Reserve Corps shall be appointed by the President and commissioned officers of the Regular Corps shall be appointed by the President with the advice and consent of the Senate.

Now, how is this resolute with HR 3200 pg. 864 "National Health Service Corps"? What might be the relation between the two?

Is this a stop-gap to prevent another FEMA failure, as seen during Katrina?

March 26 at 1:41pm

Michael Tipsword - The purpose and uses of this RRC are strictly emergency medicine in nature.

March 26 at 1:42pm

Tim Kirby - *To clarify Michael's post since it makes me look like I was spreading false info about Senate approval. The permanent corps that is confirmed has been in Existence since 1944, created by our last socialist president. I wasreferring to the new reserve corps that is Obama's hand-picked force. And he can call it up as he chooses.*

March 26 at 1:58pm

Tim Kirby - *Just remember, we will not fall overnight. But the little things that seem inconsequential will eventually equal a big thing and our way of life will disappear. Hitler did not gain all of his power overnight. And before anyone starts I am not comparing Obama to Hitler. Hitler was a fascist, Obama is a socialist. Although based on Obama's treatment of Israel they have similar feelings about Jews.*
March 26 at 2:08pm

Wesley Cramer - So few picked up on Obama's comments during the campaign about having something of a well-equipped and well trained civilian "corpse".... the exact words escaped me. It seemed absurd unless the intent was something akin to Hitler's "brown shirts" ya heh? It was almost a throwaway line but it caused a blip on my radar... one of many, kind of like the blips on the radar in the early morning hours of December 7... hmmm. May be some sort of analogy brewing here...
March 26 at 8:15pm

Tim Kirby - *What General Secretary Obama called for was "A civilian security force as well funded and equal in strength to the military." That was in the middle of '08. It stood out to me at the time as well.*
March 26 at 9:45pm

Wesley Cramer - Precisely. Sends effin shivers down my spine.... How the heck do people not hear that and say, WTW? (What The World?)
March 26 at 10:16pm

March 26, 2010 – Tim and Jim

Tim Kirby - *Just wanted to throw this out for the people who are unaware....I DO work in the health care industry.*
March 26 at 3:

Jammin' Jimmy Bean - I do volunteer work in the health care industry. Have you had a Coke and smiled yet? (^:
March 26 at 3:33pm

Tim Kirby - *That's one of your endearing qualities Jim. You practice what you preach. No coke. I had a diet Pepsi and I'm always smiling.*
March 26 at 4:11pm

Jammin' Jimmy Bean - We are two of a kind, similar in many more ways than different. Namaste.
March 26 at 4:19pm

Tim Kirby - *I guess you could say two sides of the same coin. Or maybe the left and right pages of the same book.*
March 26 at 9:52pm

March 26, 2010 – Missing Debate with a Socialist

Tim Kirby - *Hello my friends. Sorry I have been a little quiet tonight. Been dealing with a little cell phone snafu of Dean's. I hope many of you got to catch some of the spirited debate today between myself and my Socialist*

friend Michael Tipsword. Unfortunately the thread was accidentally deleted so if you missed it I am sorry. It was a good debate that settled nothing. But Michael and I had fun and we both got our message out.
March 26 at 9:49pm

Betsy Lancaster -and entertained a few others. It was interesting.....
March 26 at 11:17pm

March 27, 2010 – Red State/Blue State

Tim Kirby - *Here is a quickie I wanted to throw out to get you all thinking. When they show election maps they do the Red state, Blue state thing. Don't they have it backward? Shouldn't the states that Dems win in be the "Red" states?*
March 27 at 7:14am

Tim Kirby - *FYI, the real reason the Dem states are blue is because that is the traditional color of unions. You know, like "blue color" workers.*
March 27 at 7:14am

March 27, 2010 – Earth Hour

Tim Kirby - *Remember, tonight at 7:30 CST is "Earth Hour". They want everyone to turn off all their lights for one hour.*

If you do not believe in man-made global warming, do what I plan to do. Turn ON every light in your house and crank up your thermostat. Turn on every appliance you have. For one hour use as much energy as your house possible can.
March 27 at 12:37pm

Debra Myers Dobbs - Why would you do that?
March 27 at 1:04pm

Tim Kirby - *Hey Debra, I am not a believer of climate change. That being said, I was only making a joke. I am also not a believer of giving Ameren any more of my money that necessary.*
March 27 at 1:12pm

Penny Hanson - Tim, I love reading everyone's comments to you......I guess I know you to well....I know when you are real and feeling passionate and when the B.S. is flowing...Keep it coming.. I love reading your stuff .....makes me think, ponder, and think some more.
March 27 at 2:20pm

Debra Myers Dobbs ok - just wondered what you were thinking?
March 27 at 2:20pm

Doug Maddox - yeah, nature is not my mother...
March 27 at 8:44pm

March 29, 2010 - Hypocrisy

Tim Kirby - *Today's rant......*
March 29 at 10:05am

Lisa Hoag - issss????
March 29 at 10:14am

Tim Kirby - *I am tired of listening to the folks on the left and the State run media complaining about the actions of the evil Tea Party members. Were the slurs directed at members of Congress appropriate? No. Are the insults they have hurled at people who disagree with them appropriate? No. Is the left full of pots calling kettles black? Yes. These are the same people who spit on returning soldiers and called them baby killers when they came back from service in Vietnam. The same people who throw red paint on women in fur and call them murderers. The same people who drive spikes in trees causing chainsaws to kick back and injury loggers. The same people who set SUVs on fire at car dealers. The same people who, in the sixties, set fires and explosives on college campuses. Are the Tea Party members going too far? OK. Does the left have a leg to stand on with their holier than thou indignation? HELL NO.*
March 29 at 10:28am

March 29, 2010 – Pat Robertson

Tim Kirby - *I just read a column by Pat Robertson where he was making the same points I did this morning comparing the outcry over Tea Party slurs of congress and the radical left of the 60's and today. Before anyone else sees it and thinks I stole from Pat, I would like to point out the times. Mine was posted about 10:30 this morning. Pat's not until 7:57 tonight. Maybe he stole from me? :-)*
March 29 at 11:29pm

Tim Kirby - *Pat Robertson did point out something I was unaware of in his column. I have just accepted the incident on capitol hill with Congressmen being called the N-word and Barney Frank being called the F-word (the new F-word, not the old standby) as fact. I should have researched a little better. Turns out that even though there were TV cameras and audio recorders running all over the place during the Democrat march to the capitol, absolutely no audio or video of these supposed incidents has been produced. That seems just a little odd to me. But hey, as long as the Dems can get some political mileage out of it, who really cares if it is true or not, right? If you think I am kidding about the Dems trying to blow this thing into something that will get them votes check out this from Majority Whip James Clyburn, who accuses the Republicans IN CONGRESS of "aiding and abetting terrorism." Terrorism??? Come on Mr. Clyburn. It seems to me that the definition of terrorism is to use fear to get what you want. And what word scares more Americans*

35

than "terrorism". It seems Rep. Clyburn is the one trying to invoke fear.

And in an Op/Ed piece in today's New York Times, columnist Frank Rich made it clear that anyone who opposes the Democrats in Washington is a racist, sexist, homophobe. How about maybe we are just a bunch of people who want lower taxes. I would say that the only people making an issue of the Presidents race are the folks on the left calling all of us racist.

Also, in his article Frank Rich compares the actions of the Tea Party to "its own small-scale mimicry of Kristallnacht." How can a couple of racial slurs (if they happened at all) the wide scale destruction of synagogues and Jewish owned businesses, and the assault of Jewish women and murder of Jewish men that took place that night? How dare Frank Rich belittle the suffering of German Jews under the Nazis. THERE IS NO COMPARISON!

But, as I have said previously, the left is really showing their true feelings for the Jews so this should not come as a surprise I suppose. And for the record, Mr. Rich started out reviewing shows on Broadway for the Times, I am not sure how that qualified him to be a political writer, but hey, I guess I am not all that qualified either.

There is a lot more to be said on this, but Pat said it much more eloquently than I can so I guess I will stop here. Two rants in one day. And it's not even twof Tuesday. Dasvydanya Tovariches. (that is the pronunciation of the Russian I have been sighing off with, now you can translate it.)

March 29 at 11:58pm

March 30, 2010 – Good Friday

Tim Kirby - *One more quickie to stir it up - Davenport Iowa Renames "Good Friday" to "Spring Holiday".*
March 30 at 12:01am

Tim Kirby - *The change only lasted about a week. The people of Davenport were more than a little unhappy about the situation. The reason for the change? Best summed up by the Chairman of the committee that made the call, ""We merely made a recommendation that the name be changed to something other than Good Friday, Our Constitution calls for separation of church and state. Davenport touts itself as a diverse city and given all the different types of religious and ethnic backgrounds we represent, we suggested the change."*

Davenport Alderman Bill Edmond, "My phone has been ringing off the hook since Saturday, People are genuinely upset because this is nothing but political correctness run amok."

I agree Alderman.
March 30 at 12:05am

Bob Brown - heck they took merry Christmas away from us. Now its happy holidays or season greetings.
March 30 at 6:20am

Penny Hanson - Good for the people of Davenport....! And WE let them take away things like Merry Christmas....I will NOT say Happy Holidays instead of Merry Christmas, not matter who says it is politically correct....and Good Friday is

37

and will always be Good Friday. Keep 'em coming Tim!
March 30 at 6:52am

March 30, 2010 – Oil Drilling

Tim Kirby - *Good evening my friends. Since I, your humble narrator am the first to pile on to Obama when he is destroying our way of life, Let me also be the first to commend him when he gets it right. I just read that he is going to be making a speech in the coming week to announce that he is opening up open the Atlantic coastline, north coast of Alaska, eastern Gulf of Mexico to oil drilling.*
March 30 at 11:57pm

March 31, 2010 – Christianity Besmirched

Tim Kirby - *Hey gang, your humble narrator is slammed with work today but I had to get a couple of quickies out there.*
March 31 at 10:01am

Tim Kirby - *First, why is it that whenever the wackjobs in the Middle East are discussed it is made painfully clear that we are to distinguish between Muslims and Radical Muslims. If you ever generalize you get chastised and told not all Muslims are terrorists. I really don't have a problem with that, what I do have a problem with is not having* *that reciprocated. After the nut jobs up North were busted the week for plotting to kill cops and start a war the new has been full of stories about the "Christian militia". How about "extremist Christian militia" or "radical Christian militia"? Why is it ok to lump all Christians together but not all Muslims?*

March 31 at 10:07am

Rob Puckett - I agree!
March 31 at 10:09am

Linda Whitington - you got that right, and it's a shame
March 31 at 10:13am

Tim Kirby - *Second, and staying on religion but this time on the anti-side. Am I the only one bothered by the court decision in favor of Westburo Baptist this morning. These idiots go out and protest at soldiers funerals and spout crap at the families that there son or daughter is in hell because they were "fag-enablers" they are sick people. The father of one marine sued them for disrupting his sons funeral. Rev Phelps and his "church" counter sued saying the father was denying them their first amendment rights. An appellate court judge just said that the father has to pay the church $19000 for their legal fees. So, to summarize, he lost his son, the funeral was disrupted by nuts saying horrible things about his son, and he has to go into debt to pay them for doing it.*

I think ALL real Christians should stand up and speak out against Westburo Baptist Church and the entire Phelps family that runs it.

March 31 at 10:15am

Linda Whitington - America is leaving god out of everything and this means the good old USA is go to hell fast
March 31 at 10:22am

Tim Kirby - *Just heard that the WBC has said they plan to use the money to fund more protests. How is that for an FU to a grieving father. Lance Cpl Snyder's dad is trying to raise money to file a brief with the Supreme Court. An additional money raised over the legal fees will go to an organization for disabled veterans.*
MATTHEWSNYDER.ORG
March 31 at 10:36am

Tiffany Atkinson - I saw the dad on Fox TV yesterday and I felt so bad for him. It is terrible that we have soldiers fighting for our freedom and then you have stupid people (like the church) that go out and fight against our soldiers. I don't think this church understands how they have the freedom they do. Almost a double standards because if it wasn't for our soldiers and what America stands for then this church would not have a ground to stand on.
March 31 at 11:32am

Kelly Reese - Ok Tim...I'm lost on this subject. Why was this church protesting at this man's funeral? And just so we don't generalize...going to church does NOT make one a Christian.
March 31 at 12:31pm

Tiffany Atkinson - They were protesting because this man was a solider and fighting in the war.
March 31 at 12:33pm

Kelly Reese - That's the only reason???? Going to sound childish here, but that's dumb!! Only 2 men have ever died for me. Jesus and the American Soldier. Proud and Thankful for them both!!!
March 31 at 12:38pm

Tim Kirby - *The WBC is extremely anti-gay. The military has don't ask don't tell. Therefore Phelps and WBC believe anyone in the military is a "fag enabler" their word not mine. They have been protesting at military funerals since the war started telling parents that God wanted their sons dead because "God hates fags". They say that God has turned against America because we have tolerance for gays, that is why 9/11 happened. I have heard Shirley Phelps-Roper on the radio have small children sing anti-American songs and chants, and spouting hate. All in the name of God. Like I originally said, real Christians need to step up and denounce these folks. Whenever a soldier is killed in action they show up in mass days before the funeral to hand out fliers with the soldier's name and photo with comments that god hated him and wanted him dead. They have slogans like "God hates fags", "semper fi fags" and the one that I find most disgusting, "Thank God for dead soldiers."*
March 31 at 1:11pm

Kelly Reese - That's sick..... Ranks up there with Hitler. God loves all people...he's doesn't love what all people do. And I believe in the end, He will have final judgment.
March 31 at 1:16pm

Tim Kirby - *It's funny you should mention Hitler. The WBC is also a noted anti-Semitic group. They protested the opening of the National Holocaust museum with Fred Phelps stating "Jews are the real Nazis" they are holocaust deniers saying any suffering of the Jews was probably miniscule.*

The also protest at the funerals of gay murder victims, taunting their families. The say that Catholicism and Islam are devil worship.

Shirley Phelps-Roper even went so far as to say in a documentary that the $200000 they spend annually to go protest is money spent to spread "God's hate".

Pretty screwed up, right. And for people not too familiar with Christianity, these are the people they see on their TV screens, so they think this is what it is all about
March 31 at 1:46pm

Kelly Reese - So this SP-Roper chick is spreading "God's Hate" as a good thing??? Now how messed up is that and how many people is she messing up???
March 31 at 1:49pm

Tim Kirby - *Luckily they only have 71 members, mostly Phelps family members. The real problem is that their actions get so much media coverage. And the actions are so deplorable.*
March 31 at 2:04pm

Tim Kirby - *Man, it's scary that I am on the same page as Michael Moore on this one.*
March 31 at 2:05pm

March 31, 2010 – Drilling Correction

Tim Kirby - *Dear readers, it seems your humble narrator has misspoke this morning. The only new drilling will be off the coast of Virginia.*
March 31 at 12:19pm

Tim Kirby - *Alaska and the Gulf are still going to be verboten. AND while everyone is rejoicing over the crumbs being doled out by General Secretary Obama, he is planning on cramming through his job killing, energy depleting Cap and Tax plan. I should have known when I posted that this morning that it was too good to be true, that he might actually be planning on doing the right thing for a change.*
March 31 at 12:23pm

Jammin' Jimmy Bean - I'm NOT debating, but you are WAY off on this one. Maybe you should re-check your facts.
April 1 at 11:04am

Tim Kirby - *Nope, facts checked and rechecked, drilling 50 miles off of Virginia IF it passes environmental and military checks. Alaska and the Gulf, he is willing to allow exploration, not actual drilling, there will be no new lease sales until 2012, if at all. He also blocked all exploration along the West coast, which was green lighted in 2008 by the Dem controlled Congress. He closed a lot more doors than he opened. It was a calculated feint, a pretense to disarm everyone before the cap and tax legislation comes up, nothing more. The proposal for the FL Gulf coast is blocked by an existing moratorium that Congress will not*

43

let expire. He actually cancelled plans for Bristol Bay in Alaska, and reversed a decision from last year to open up parts of the Chukchi and Beaufort seas. It was all a big smoke screen for the announcement coming later today on oppressive emissions and fuel economy standards that will further damage the already sagging auto industry. The new standards, 35.5 mpg on all new cars, will add an estimated $1300 per vehicle.

April 1 at 11:53am

April 1, 2010 – Arctic Ice

Tim Kirby - *Global warming continues to unravel. A report today shows Arctic ice back to "normal" level for the first time in 9 years.*

April 1 at 12:23pm

Tim Donaldson - Don't tell the lib's!!!   Wouldn't matter anyway...............it's just more lies, meant to obfuscate the "TRUTH",   April 1 at 8:47pm

April 1, 2010 – Rhode Island Flood

Tim Kirby - *I have a question.*

April 1 at 12:35pm

Tim Kirby - *We have listened to the media and folks on the left complain that the Bush administration did not respond quickly enough, or strongly enough to the Katrina flooding*

in New Orleans. To listen to the media Bush blew up the dykes himself. Rosie O'Donnell, wackbag that she is, just brought it up again on her blog this week.

So my question is this, why are we not hearing in outrage about the fact that Obama has yet to visit or even mention the flooding in Rhode Island. RI is already struggling economically, and the massive flooding is going to hurt them for years to come. Maybe you are not aware that there is even a problem because it is not being covered too much. What it tells me is that the left didn't really care all that much about NO it was just something to use against Bush. I have to believe though that the people of RI have the same rights as the people of NO.
April 1 at 12:42pm

Holly Tipsword - I haven't even heard of RI flooding!!
April 1 at 1:22pm

Tim Kirby - *It is so bad that they had to close interstate 95 because it is under water. But it is hardly being covered. The only reason I found out how bad things are is because two days ago our corporate officers flooded and took down phones and computers nationwide.*
April 1 at 1:42pm

Tiffany Atkinson - Fox news has some coverage on it...it looks really bad
April 1 at 3:13pm

Michael Tipsword - It IS bad! And I'm frankly disappointed the response time has been so poor. Maybe the poor response time is bureaucratic in nature, so regardless of

who's in power it's gonna suck until we can immediately and expeditiously mobilize massive amounts of aid at a moment's notice.
April 2 at 10:05am

April 2, 2010 – Obama's Hurt Feelings

Tim Kirby - *Poor, abused Obama want his critics to "tone down the rhetoric", he ain't seen nothing yet. Furthermore, if had had to endure the comments that Bush did for eight years it would drive him to drink. Oh wait a minute, I forgot, Obama DOES have drunken frat parties in the White House. It was Bush, a recovering alcoholic, who maintained his sobriety under extreme pressure.*
April 2 at 10:38am

Jammin' Jimmy Bean - Of course G Dub had nothing to do with the comments that came his way. He was the best president we ever had...........who was brain-dead! Yup, you got me back at it.
April 2 at 10:41am

Michael Tipsword - Did he maintain his sobriety? There's evidence he fell off the wagon, and this reported in multiple sources, so let's not attack the messenger or accuse the source of being "suspect":   Many accuse Bush of being not so smart, and while that may be true, maybe we should really just express kind pity toward him, considering how he was manipulated and etc. by his Daddy's Big $$$ friends,

Cheney & his Big $$$ friends, etc.
April 2 at 11:06am

Tim Kirby - *Now Jim, you know I have NEVER said the Bush 43 was a great president. In fact, I am pretty sure you know I was not even a fan. I was merely pointing out that Obama complaining about criticism was kind of silly when you compare to what his predecessors had to deal with. He has not come close to being trashed the way the left trashed Bush or the right trashed Clinton. If he cannot handle the animosity maybe he went into the wrong line of work. He is kind of being a big baby about it.*

As far as did or didn't Bush fall off the wagon, none of us will ever know for sure, staying up on that wagon is hard to do (I only know of a handful, including a close personal friend who I will respect with anonymity, that have managed to stay up there without slipping) even under the best of circumstances, let alone when dealing with that kind of pressure. But either way he did not have the drunken parties with his friends in the White House.

And Jim, you are too much like me, I knew you couldn't stay on the sidelines.
April 2 at 11:32am

Michael Tipsword - Maybe, just maybe, Obama thinks that the consequences of such rhetoric hurt progress. I doubt his lil' feelings are hurt by the big, bag republicans...
April 2 at 11:42am

Jammin' Jimmy Bean - I know someone very close who worked with Obama when he was a Senator, and I've been told he's MUCH TOUGHER than he appears. He makes our

47

country look so much better to the rest of the world than G Dub did and that alone makes him a better president IMHO.
April 2 at 11:52am

Michael Tipsword - At least he's not inciting hatred of the US worldwide like Bush & Co. did.
April 2 at 11:53am

Michael Tipsword - Reconciliation & communication with nations throughout the world is the key to it, I think.
April 2 at 11:56am

Tim Kirby - *Unfortunately, when you are the leader of the free world appearance is everything. And of course he is not inciting hatred around the world, he kowtows to every foreign leader he meets, except of course our friends like Netanyahu. Regardless of if he is week or only appears week, he definitely is not making our enemies nervous.*

But my main point when I started this was about the whining. In the last 40 years I have seen a lot of presidents get criticized badly, but he is the first I have seen go on TV and say everyone should be nicer to him.
April 2 at 12:03pm

Michael Tipsword - Can you provide a quote, or something, so I can investigate?
April 2 at 12:23pm

Michael Tipsword - The only thing I can find is "The president said both Democrats and Republicans have a responsibility to tone down the rhetoric, but that much of it has to do with the current media environment in which

extreme comments are echoed in the blogosphere." Which is a far cry from "be nicer to me".
April 2 at 12:26pm

Michael Tipsword - Can I get some source or a quote that indicates he stated something, anything to the effect of Obama saying "be nicer to me"?
April 2 at 1:30pm

Tim Kirby - *You have the right piece from CBS, but you need to read the entire thing to get the context. He was referring directly to the right wing talkers harsh criticism, where he refers to the "vitriol" from the right. I do not believe that I said be nicer was a direct quote. I was merely characterizing his comments. When you listen to the entire piece in context it has a different overall meaning than if you just read the one quote with the token bipartisan line.*
April 2 at 1:43pm

Michael Tipsword - "... but he is the first I have seen go on TV and say everyone should be nicer to him."
April 2 at 1:45pm

Tim Kirby - *As I said, that was my characterization of the tone of his comments and I stand by it. It was not a direct quote or it would have had quotation marks around it. Feel free to peruse my previous posts, you will notice that when I quote someone I make it obvious and credit the source.*
April 2 at 1:58pm

Michael Tipsword - But asking both sides to tone down the rhetoric is a far cry from saying "be nicer to me".
April 2 at 2:00pm

Michael Tipsword - He still doesn't appear to be taking the stance of victim, not is he whining, etc. I agree with what he says, the vitriol coming from the Right Wing talking heads is not constructive, and so much of it is downright lies! (see that FactCheck.org article).
April 2 at 2:10pm

Tim Kirby - *I am going to stand by my characterization.*
April 2 at 3:32pm

Lisa Hoag - OMG!!!! Are you lefties really so up the big O's ass that you have to be technical like my 18yr old daughter, on what EXACTLY he said???? I don't think that was nearly as twisted as he and his cronies twist our constitutions meaning!!! I love it.....please continue to make excuses for him LMFAO! I need some more laughs throughout the day! BAAAHAAAHAAA!!!
April 2 at 4:45pm

Michael Tipsword - Wow... Let it all hang out Lisa! Don't hide that light under a bushel basket.
    You mentioned being 'technical'. I think you meant 'precise'. I don't see anything wrong with being precise, it keeps one from sounding like a fool (not meaning you, Tim). Anyone can make generalizations, but I won't dumb myself down as easily as some do. I am making excuses for no one, I'm just attentive and intelligent enough to understand what he means when he says things. If I was intellectually

lazy enough to desire that someone else think for me, I'd get a lobotomy and watch Bill O'Reilly & Glen Beck, then finish it off with some Rush Limbaugh.

I'm happy I can provide entertainment in between episodes of Hee-Haw and Green Acres.

A few questions for you, Lisa:

1. How are Obama and 'his cronies' twisting the meaning of the Constitution?
2. Can define, exactly, what it means to be "up the Big O's ass"?.

Have a great day1
April 2 at 5:27pm

Tim Kirby - *Uh oh.....*
April 2 at 5:41pm

Michael Tipsword - Hey, Tim, you and I were in the midst of an intelligent conversation, then someone butted in, without saying anything intelligent at all. That's it & that's all.
April 2 at 6:07pm

Lisa Hoag - Whatever you say Mr. Intelligence. Since you're so smart you figure out what it means. LMAO! Have fun trying to bash on me, your arrogance is just adding to my entertainment! C'mon got some more for me since you know me so well!! LOL! Let it all go I can take it!!!! Ahhhaha!
April 2 at 6:13pm

Michael Tipsword - OK, here's an attempt to explain it myself, correct me if I am wrong:

1. You believe HR3200 is illegal as it is counter to the US Constitution
2. Being up the Big O's ass means we're either sucking up to him or supporting him

Arrogance? I'm sorry if I gave you that impression. The medium of the Internet (the written word) is easy to misunderstand, without many of the other forms of feedback we have in spoken conversation: tones of voice, facial expressions and body language. I admit have confidence in my positions and opinions, and feel passionate about many issues. Sometimes this will run to the tune of drawing out the CW of/from others, even on issues I care little about, even from those whose positions I don't necessarily agree with.

As Tim can attest, I make every effort to back up my claims, posits and points with real information, actual facts. I attempt to "lead a horse to water", mainly providing access to information, without ramming it down someone's throat (unless I am super-stoked about a subject), leaving it up to their motivation to learn. I believe "The truth will set you free", and everyone should not rely upon anyone to think for them, all it requires is some investigation, reading, & processing of information.

Back to facts. I have been made to understand these 'facts' often make some angry. Some facts make me angry, too.

Nope, I'm pretty sure I don't know you.

Happy Friday!!!!

-mikey
April 2 at 7:04pm

Lisa Hoag - LOL! I gotta go get me sum more straw to pick my tooth with!
April 2 at 8:31pm

Michael Tipsword - I am sorry about the nasty hee-haw & green acres comment. srsly. that was low, and uncalled for. my apologies.
April 2 at 10:19pm

Michael Tipsword - Yeah, I deleted my omgwtfbbq comment. still, omgwtfbbq.
April 2 at 10:21pm

Greg Peace - W was a retard. He didn't run this country his staff did. Cutting taxes for corp. and the top 2% didn't make life in the country any better. War weather just or unjust cost more than what most realize. I have family members fighting it. Do you? My family has lost more than you even know. We spend more on a war on fronts then what would cost to regulate healthcare. It's not Obamacare Its realty. Get on the wagon. Quit acting like a right wing person that believes your 7.00 dollars runs a nation.
April 3 at 12:22am

Lisa Hoag - I'm thinking you're referencing Tim not me, but just in case yes, my little brother was in Iraq when the statue fell. He was shot @ by RPG's and was a grunt morterman. HE, may I add is a conservative that didn't care

for W but HATES the O-man.
April 3 at 3:14am

Tim Kirby - *We are not supposed to use the R-word anymore. It is the one derogatory word that the left still seems okay with. Can't defame any other group, but the mentally challenged are no problem, just look at the beating poor little Trig Palin takes. Even if you hat his mom,. it's not his fault. So until, the n-word and the f-word are okay, lets avoid the r-word.*

2nd, You do not reach the level of evening running for President with some level of intellect. And surrounding yourself with good people is one of the smartest things you can do. Then you don't have someone like Joe Biden putting his foot in your mouth over and over. Or Rahm Emanuel spouting his idiocy at every turn.

I have several family members in the military, some in Iraq, some in Afghanistan. Army, Marines and Navy. But you know what, last time I checked they all volunteered to serve. In fact, as I think about it, our entire military is volunteer. And since the military is who fights when there is a war, all of those volunteers knew when they enlisted that they may have to fight.

Yes, war is expensive but so is the alternative, losing everything we, as a nation hold dear.

It IS Obamacare. It IS Socialism. It IS un-American. It WAS passed in violation of the Constitution. It DOES violate the Constitution. Nowhere in the Constitution does it say that government can FORCE you do buy something (i.e. health insurance). The provisions of the bill are designed to force insurance companies out of business and

54

set up an eventual single payer system with the government running the show.

I am not acting like a "right wing person", I AM a "right wing person."

I pay a hell of a lot more than $7.00 dollars in taxes. But even if that was all I paid, it would be too much. Forgive me for wanting to keep the money I earn to spend on my family and not the families of others.

What happened to the American Dream? When you worked hard to pull yourself up and make a better life instead of just waiting around to get something for nothing.

I read this quote the other day about those of us in the Boomer generation, and I think it sums it all up." My generation could well be the first generation in American history to leave our country worse off than we found it." - Nancy Morgan
April 3 at 10:29am

Greg Peace - I understand what you are saying Tim. I also agree. However, I also believe healthcare should be a right not a privilege. I want to do away with caps. Pre-existing conditions. I want to know if I get sick my coverage will take care of me and not bankrupt me. We live in America. We like to help those less fortunate in other countries. Let's try taking care of our own first.
April 3 at 12:41pm

Michael Tipsword - I agree with Greg. I do not want anyone's good, working, adequate plan to be changed either. I think this bill is going to see massive changes in the

next four years.
April 3 at 2:40pm

Tim Kirby - *I have been perusing my copy of the US Constitution, and for the life of me, I cannot find the section that deals with the right of equal health coverage for all. Nor, can I find the section dealing with the government forcing someone to buy a product or service against their will. Perhaps someone could show me where that is at so I can read it over. This country was founded on the principle that hard work pays off. I understand that there are a few people who are truly unable to work, and those folks already have options like SS and Medicare/Medicaid. We are talking now about giving people who choose not to try for success rewards for their lack of effort.*

As to pre-existing conditions, let's say you go in for car insurance and the agent asks when you would like the policy to start. You tell him right away because you were in an accident last night and totaled the car. Or how about, you go in for homeowners insurance the day after your house burns down, I am guessing in both cases you will be shown the door. It is the same with health insurance. Go through life carrying little or no insurance and then get have a heart attack or cancer and opt for the better policy now.

And the people that have succeeded and are now paying for the so called "Cadillac plans" are going to be punished for their success. They are getting huge taxes placed on their premiums. There is some incentive to get ahead.

The big talking point is babies not getting coverage because they are born with a health condition. If the parents have insurance, the child is added to the plan before birth and any subsequent conditions are there for covered. Where the problem lays is with people having babies without insurance. My thought there is, having kids is expensive so if you can't afford them, buy a condom.

As far as the uninsured in a medical emergency, hospitals have to treat, by law.

I also wouldn't mind keeping some of that foreign aid right here at home. This country is on the verge of bankruptcy and our value on the world market is dropping faster than I can type this. If we don't slow the spending, there is going to be nothing left. What this HC bill does to the deficit could very well be the straw that broke the camel's back as far as the economy is concerned.

But that is what the left in Washington really wants anyway, isn't it. Tear it down so they can rebuild a new Marxist government on the ashes.

April 3 at 4:36pm

April 2, 2010 – Obama's Census

Tim Kirby - *My census form said the lying on the form was punishable by law. Is Obama going to be prosecuted for lying? The white house issued a statement in response to questions that Obama checked African-American under race. That is a falsehood. He has a white mother. As someone of mixed parentage, he should have checked*

other and then specified his 50/50 mixed race status.
April 2 at 1:54pm

Tim Kirby - *Before everyone piles on, this is NOT about race. It is about honesty and integrity. I will not respond to any calls of racism. I will only comment on discussions of the honesty factor.*
April 2 at 1:56pm

Holly Tipsword - At least you got your form!
April 2 at 2:06pm

Rob Puckett - BILLY JOEL SINGS IT WELL,,,,,,, HONESTY,,,,,, such a lonely word.
April 2 at 2:29pm

Michael Tipsword - Well, can a person on the street differentiate that a light-skinned black man is half white? Not really. Society will label you with whatever race it 'appears' you are, despite reality. We Anthropologists call this "Hypo descent". So, if he feels society would call him a black man, it's easy to see why he wouldn't check 'other'.
April 2 at 4:31pm

Tim Kirby - *As I said, it is not about race, it is about HONESTLY filling out the form. How he views himself is not the question. The question was "What is your race?" He did not answer honestly.*
April 2 at 4:35pm

Rob Puckett - WELL TIM ,,,,,,,,,it was half true. Lol
April 2 at 5:00pm

Penny Hanson - I have been on the soap box you on about Obama all along... he is 50/50.....NOT an African American.... call it like it really is.....as you said Honestly!!!!
April 2 at 5:47pm

Michael Tipsword - On census forms, the government depends on individuals' self-identification. Due in part to a centuries-old history within the United States, historical experiences pre- and post-slavery, and migrations throughout North America, contemporary African Americans possess varying degrees of admixture with European ancestry. A lesser percentage also have Native American ancestry.
April 3 at 1:04am

Tim Kirby - *But Obama has more than a varying degree of European ancestry. His father was from Kenya, no European blood at all there. His mom was Caucasian, no idea of her exact background. That is a 50/50 mix of race and falls firmly in "other/mulatto." It just is what it is. He was dishonest on the form and no amount of verbal jousting and semantics will change that. We are not talking about someone like myself who has Jew, Native American, and Scots-Irish ancestors. They are all so far back that the bloodlines have diluted down. We are talking about first generation. I think I am going to be done with this topic, because as a Conservative, I am getting real close to being labeled a racist. Everyone else feel free to continue, but I am going to quit before I have to defend myself from spurious charges.*
April 3 at 10:40am

59

Tim Kirby - *I have to jump back in one more time in the interest of full disclosure. I am 1/4 Jew, 1/8 Native American, and the rest an assortment of Europeans. I would qualify as a Native American if I maintained a tribal affiliation, which I do not. I am eligible for Israeli citizenship under the "Law of Return" which I do not plan to exercise. Since the Native American is so far back, and I don't maintain affiliation, I am justified in not mentioning it on the form. For the purposes of the census, Jew is considered Caucasian. I just wanted this on the record before someone decided to call me a hypocrite. Now I am really moving on from this thread before the accusations start to fly.*
April 3 at 10:52am

April 2, 2010 – Obama's Approval Rating

Tim Kirby - *CBS news has released the latest Presidential approval numbers for Obama. April 2009 69% Approval April 2010 44% Approval That is down 5 points since the end of March. Looks like maybe it isn't just those on the far right that are unhappy about Obama Socialism*
April 2 at 4:40pm

Michael Tipsword - Likely the result of the rhetoric and nastiness being thrown about.
April 2 at 4:48pm

Tim Kirby - *C'mon Michael, you're reaching a little on that one*. :-)
April 2 at 5:15pm

Michael Tipsword - Well, maybe... Alright, I concede.
April 2 at 6:03pm

April 3, 2010 – Birther Debate

Tim Kirby - via Jeff Bebar:

Exclusive: Highly Decorated Army Surgeon Lt. Col. Terry Lakin Refuses All Military Orders Until Obama

HOME > PUBLICATIONS > Exclusive: Highly Decorated Army Surgeon Lt. Col. Terry Lakin Refuses All Military Orders Until Obama Proves He Is a Natural Born Citizen
April 3 at 5:01pm

Michael Tipsword - Wow... I did not know there were really anyone left clinging to the "Birther" ideas. The idea that Obama is not a US citizen?

It seems ignorant to continue to beat a dead horse. I understand that deep-seated bigotry among Conservatives/Republicans motivated these fringe ideas early on (how dare we have an African-American president), but the issue has been laid to rest, and long ago!

Now, if there is justice, this Lt. Col. will be busted down at the least, and forced to mobilize. From the perspective of the military, this SHOULD be disrespect of the worst kind, as

61

it's directed at the Commander in Chief.
April 5 at 11:15am

Tim Kirby - *I would argue that the citizenship is open to debate and that is no one's fault but Obama. Why does he refuse to present an actual birth certificate. The certificate of live birth that he has produced is not the same thing. Also a lot of people in Kenya claim he was born there, including his own grandmother, who died shortly after asserting so. All he has to do is produce the document and it all goes away. It has nothing to do with being African-American, I would say the same thing if his father was from England. Besides, he is not African American, he is mullato.*

I am not saying he is not native born, I am just saying end the debate, provide the document.

As for the officer, yes he should deploy, but he has a point, he produced his birth cert. Why can't the Commander in Chief do the same. And IF Obama is not qualified to be pres. By the constitution the any orders from him would be invalid. But, we all know how Obama and his ilk feel about the constitution
April 5 at 11:39am

Michael Tipsword - Mulatto is considered derogatory as it stems from a Spanish word for Mule (half horse, half donkey). Yes, Obama is African American by definition. It is not up to a group (any group, however defined) to define Obama's ethnicity or heritage, it is up to Obama and his ethnic peers (African-Americans). Many conservatives will choose to split hairs on this, when in similar situations they would not stick to a consistent principle. I have already provided the information on hypo descent, and the classification of African-American. I don't see any reason why I would have to do it again.... Is the information I provided to dense for Conservatives to understand?

How do you think Obama feels about the US Constitution, or are you making assumptions? Hell, W cursed and said the Constitution was "just a damned piece of paper".

April 5 at 11:52am

Tim Kirby - *I treat you with respect and must demand you do the same. It is the same old tactic of the left. When you are losing on the facts switch to the insults. I too have went over the info repeatedly and am tired of doing so. Obama's mother was white thus he is as white as he is black. First mixed president just doesn't sound as good for the history books. That is not subjective, it is not up to an individual to define their ethnicity. It is simple genetics.*

Please provide context and source for Bush quote. Obama showed his disdain for the Constitution when he signed the HC bill which was passed in violation of the Constitution. The reconciliation procedure is for budget bills only, not to subvert the Constitution provision for filibuster.

April 5 at 12:14pm

Tim Kirby - *It was also an Obama crony that said in Quincy last week, "I don't care about the constitution" and if you look back through my posts you will find the video, so you have my source and the complete context, unlike your one*

line from bush.
April 5 at 12:19pm

Tim Kirby - *There is really nothing as sweet as using someone's own weapon against them. I know why you did not provide a source or context for your Bush quote. Because there is none. You are merely spreading a leftist lie created to discredit Bush. I researched this myself since you would not provide info and found multiple sites refuting this ever was said. I knew you wouldn't believe any site that I visit so how about one of yours, fact check also says nope. This appeared on Capitol Blue known for false reporting. So perhaps this would be a good time for you to retract your statement.*
April 5 at 1:07pm

Michael Tipsword - We're not losing on the facts, hell, it seems like a pissing contest.

If a group or person decides to ignore evidence, quite concrete evidence, then what else am I supposed to think? As a social scientist I understand that while Obama is of mixed heritage, he can and would claim African-American, as his heritage DOES fit that definition. African-American does not mean you have no other ethnic heritage BUT black, in fact many A-A's have native American, European, Latino, etc. heritage, some they may not even be aware of. The info is out there, but when you choose to ignore facts, I can't help you. What else is it going to take to convince you of the viability of his choice to characterize himself as African-American?

If a group continues to harp upon a point already disproven, that group should expect accusations of stupidity. Actually it should be ignorance, but at this point I'm not obliged to be specific.

Here's info on that statement Bush made on The Constitution, I thought it was incredibly well-known, so I did not think you would have trouble finding info on it.
April 5 at 2:01pm

Tim Kirby - *You better reread the fact check site. It says the info is incorrect. In fact Capitol Hill Blue has removed it as well and it was their story. At this point I have to believe you are disseminating false information on purpose to aid your position. It does not matter how many times you say it, it is not going to be true. I even used a left leaning website to prove the accusations false.*

As for Obama, to go back to the original topic, until I see a birth certificate I think we better go with Kenyan African. And I suppose you are right, a white south African who moves here and has kids would be African American. But he isn't black, no matter what he checked on a census form. And THAT is not subjective, that is genetics! I can call myself a ham sandwich, but that doesn't make me one

And once again, I ask for the same respect I show you.
April 5 at 2:18pm

Michael Tipsword - Yes, it claims the incident was unlikely to have happened. My bad, you win that one.

I believe the "Birther" position has been dis-proven long ago. From that Snopes article: "The Fourteenth Amendment states that "all persons born or naturalized in the United

65

States , and subject to the jurisdiction thereof, are citizens of the United States". Since Hawaii is part of the US, even if Obama's parents were both non-US citizens who hadn't even set foot in the country until just before he was born, he'd still qualify as a natural born citizen."

And here's the birth certificate: <link removed>
April 5 at 3:00pm

Michael Tipsword - Sorry for implying that the information was too dense for conservative minds, but at that point the blatant denial of the truth was incredibly frustrating.
April 5 at 3:04pm

Tim Kirby - *You have posted the problem. That is not a State of Hawaii birth certificate. That is a certificate of live birth. There is a difference. That can be given to babies born in Hawaii or children that move to the islands and need id for government purposes. Obama has said repeatedly that he does have an actual Hawaiian birth cert. But has up to now refused to produce it. That is the rub, if he would just produce it, the whole thing would go away. And naturalized as per the fourteenth doesn't get it for president. It is clearly stated he must be naturally born. You are right about children of foreign parents born on American soil. That's what happens when illegals have kids here. The kids are citizens and the parents subject to deportation. With Obama there is also the problem of relatives and government officials in Kenya saying they we present at the birth in Kenya. Again, all he has to do is provide a real certified Birth Certificate and it all goes*

away.
April 5 at 3:11pm

April 5, 2010 – Obama's Long Answer

Tim Kirby - *Obama appears to be losing his mind. At a Q&A last week a woman commented that "We are over taxed as it is." Obama's response? A rambling, hard to follow, 2500 word, 17 minute reply that wandered from topic to topic*
April 5 at 8:10am

Jeff Bebar - Why doesn't he just spill the beans he wants to disarm and control us. He'd probably still have a 30 percent approval rating and 2 and a half years to convince another 21 percent through handouts, bullying, and the state medias!
April 5 at 8:18am

Jammin' Jimmy Bean - Quick, let's move to Costa Rica with Rush. You guys go first and I'll turn off the lights.
April 5 at 8:32am

Tim Kirby - *Jim, I am more of a Belize guy myself. No extradition treaty with US and you can get citizenship and a passport in the name of your choosing just by opening a small bank account. Don't ask how I know that, it isn't important for the purposes of our conversation.*
April 5 at 8:55am

67

Jammin' Jimmy Bean - I'll be right behind you, don't get nervous if it takes a while, look how long people have been waiting for Jesus.
April 5 at 9:07am

Jammin' Jimmy Bean - A small bank account is the only type I could open! (^:
April 5 at 9:07am

Tim Kirby - *Not sure how we got here from Obama being unable to give a concise answer to a simple comment, but, since we are, the truth is, if I ever really did decide to leave the country (not gonna happen) I would go to Israel. The care about defense, they support the principles we used to, and I can exercise the "law of return" and get my citizenship by just stepping off the plane. In all honesty, I have thought several times about doing just that and maintaining dual citizenship.*
April 5 at 9:26am

Tim Donaldson - Jim, are you comparing yourself to Jesus, the son of GOD!!??

You do kinda look like some of the pictures I've seen of him.
April 5 at 1:23pm

Jammin' Jimmy Bean - No comparison, I can verify my existence. (^: (Here we go!)
April 5 at 1:34pm

Tim Kirby - *Can you? How do I know that you are not a figment of my imagination? Or perhaps I am a figment of*

yours.
April 5 at 1:46pm

April 5, 2010 – Upside Down Guam

Tim Kirby - *Somehow I managed to miss Rep. Hank Johnson last week saying he was afraid that building a new Naval base on Guam would put so many people on the island that it would tip over and capsize. This is one of the people deciding our future. Fyi he voted yes on the health care bill*
April 5 at 9:46am

Jeff Bebar - The answer from the admiral, and the look on his face was awesome! However, I would have waited a minute and asked the Con-man "is that a joke, isn't there supposed to be a punch line?"
April 5 at 10:04am

Tara Huchel-nestich - Yes I heard this ! I have met him ! Sorry to say he is a rep from my beautiful GA ! I'm totally embarrassed for my state and for my country !!!
April 5 at 11:58am

April 5, 2010 - Obsession

Tim Kirby - *I just heard Obama reading green eggs and ham on Easter. It even sounded like a campaign speech in*

69

his delivery.
April 5 at 12:34pm

Jammin' Jimmy Bean - I think you're obsessed. I also think if our president found the cure for cancer, ended all wars, and had everybody in the world working you would still find fault. Why didn't you spend this much time criticizing G Dub when he was dragging our country through the mud? It's beginning to seem like you're not concerned so much about our country doing better as you are with our president doing worse. Kinda like that one dude on the radio whose parents named him after the greatest rock band in Canadian history.
April 5 at 12:51pm

Tim Kirby - *Have you heard the clip? It sounds like either a campaign speech or a Southern Baptist revival. I've been to both so I know the sound. Yes I am obsessed, with this country maintaining the values that made it great, and Obama, Pelosi, et al are doing their level best to destroy that, so that they can build on the ashes. I did criticize Bush repeatedly for his fiscal policy. Unlike the left I do not follow in lock step with my parties candidate. If he is blowing it I will step up and say so. I do not wish Obama to do worse. I would love for him to do better, but completely rearranging the things that made this country great is not doing better. I am not alone in this, his approval numbers are at 44% (half of what Bush was at the same point in his presidency), that means even a large portion of the people that voted for him now have buyer's remorse.*

As far as obsession, you seem to have a little of that going on today, this is the second time you have mentioned Limbaugh and you have been mentioning him a lot lately, he must be getting under your skin just a wee bit. As far as my postings I'll tell ya what I will do, read my next status update.
April 5 at 1:19pm

Kim S Coon - you tell them Tim. I agree with you!!!!
April 5 at 1:41pm

Tim Kirby - *Hey Jim, as you know, I lost mom last year to cancer. It is pretty far-fetched, but if he did find the cure, I would not only vote for him in 2012 I would go do to door for him.*
April 5 at 4:28pm

April 5, 2010 - Machiavelli

Tim Kirby - *Someone commented on one of my posts last week and said at least Obama wasn't inspiring hatred around the world "like Bush," so my question is why did Hamid Karzai threaten to join the Taliban over his and his countries treatment by the Obama regime?*
April 5 at 12:42pm

Jammin' Jimmy Bean - Let me guess.......because Obama is the anti-Christ, no wait, he (Karzai) should like that. Another guess..........because Obama wants to take all our guns away and enslave us to do his dirty work, wait, he would like that

71

too. Another guess............ because he (Karzai) is crazier
than a shit house rat.
April 5 at 12:58pm

Tim Kirby - *I was only pointing out the inaccuracy of
Michael Tipsword's post from last week.*
April 5 at 1:08pm

Michael Tipsword - The CW is that Karzai is not serious, nor
pandering to pro-Taliban members of parliament. It has
been noted that Karzai has been behaving erratically lately,
and this could be nothing more than bizarre behavior. At
the most nefarious, Karzai is probably making such a drastic
threat in response to foreign meddling in Afghan affairs,
specifically the calls for reform of the Afghan government.
The criticism stems from supposed foreign interference with
elections last year - elections some characterize as
fraudulent. I concede that those who interfered may not
have been officially representing the US, may have been
CIA, of which the US Gov't would not necessarily have
known about. Similar lack of coordination (CIA and official
gov't) has caused problems in the past.

On a larger note, there is a long train of US interference
that has been happening in Afghanistan since 2001 (and
even earlier), it's nothing new.
April 5 at 2:45pm

Tim Kirby - *The foreign interference is exactly the reason.
He is also unhappy that Obama will not take a harder
stance on Iran because a nuclear Iran is a threat to
Afghanistan. This was said in a meeting of government
officials, not a press conference. I was simply pointing out*

that not every world leader is a fan of the policies of Obama. Netanyahu is not a big fan either.
April 5 at 3:18pm

Tim Kirby - *As far as the world loves Obama, the world though Bush was a warmonger, "it is better to be feared than loved, if you can't be both" - Niccolo Machiavelli*
April 5 at 3:23pm

Jammin' Jimmy Bean - I'm not sure who Niccolo is, but I have lived my life according to that philosophy.
April 5 at 3:28pm

Tim Kirby - *Niccolo di Bernardo dei Machiavelli, 1469-1527 Known as the Father of Modern Political Theory. Politician and later, after the restoration of the Medici and his removal from public service, an author. Known for his work, The Prince. The main theme of which is, that all means may be resorted to for the establishment and preservation of authority -- the end justifies the means -- and that the worst and most treacherous acts of the ruler are justified by the wickedness and treachery of the governed.*
April 5 at 4:22pm

April 5, 2010 – To Post or Not To Post

Tim Kirby - *Someone just basically told me that I text to much political stuff. If everyone feels that way then I will stop. So now I leave it up to you, my friends to decide if I*

rave politically or if I stop. My fate is in your hands. (By the way my left leaning chum, if I quit, you quit)
April 5 at 1:23pm

Kim S Coon - keep going
April 5 at 1:39pm

Jammin' Jimmy Bean - That's a deal I could easily and honestly keep. Namaste.
April 5 at 1:41pm

Angie Ruwe - rave on!
April 5 at 1:47pm

Tiffany Atkinson - Well Tim if they don't like it they could always take you off the friends list and then they won't have to see it....I say more people need to know what is going on in America today...not enough read the news-paper, watch the news, or study what America is about the function of our county...so keep it up
April 5 at 1:49pm

Tara Huchel-nestich - No please don't !
April 5 at 2:02pm

Jammin' Jimmy Bean - Let the bashing continue!
April 5 at 2:20pm

Tim Kirby - *Jim, you truly are the yin to my Yang. Or the Laurel to my Hardy. You are every bit as hooked on politics as I am brother. Namaste*
April 5 at 2:30pm

Jammin' Jimmy Bean - GUILTY as charged. I really do CARE.
April 5 at 2:38pm

Terri Collins Heath - I would fear for your health & safety
were you to hold it all in... Let it rip & the FB world can
choose to read, skim or skip.
April 5 at 3:07pm

Michael Tipsword - No sweat, man. No sweat.
April 5 at 3:26pm

Joseph Doggett - hell with the government they are all
crooked say what u want idc this world has enough
problems of its own they want to help out everybody else
what about us the American people
April 5 at 3:40pm

Tim Kirby - *Thanks everyone. Sorry Jim, but let's be honest,
neither of us could every really quit. We are too passionate
about our beliefs. If we didn't care, we would probably be
a lot happier.*
April 5 at 4:24pm

April 6, 2010 – Nuclear Strategy?

Tim Kirby *It is something new EVERYDAY with this
administration.*

*I just read Obama is revamping our nuclear strategy. He is
making the blanket statement that will NOT use nuclear
weapons against a non-nuclear state, even for defense in*

75

the event of a crippling bio or chemical attack. Those
weapons are to be a deterrent, if you tell our enemies we
won't use them, I don't think they will be deterred.
Especially since we will not retaliate in kind either. This just
after Russia and Venezuela announce an arms deal. He is
doing everything he can to undermine out security. I guess
next he will tell our enemies we will not use guns if the
invade us.
April 6 at 6:33am

Penny Hanson - My theory....they attack us....blow them to
pieces... lol but I guess the USA won't continue to be the
powerhouse we have been in the past huh?
April 6 at 4:15pm

April 6, 2010 – START Update

Tim Kirby - *A related story to my earlier post.*

I just read some of the details of the new START treaty
with Russia. Not good. We have always negotiated from
strength, not anymore. Obama has backed out on missile
defense in Poland and the Czech Republic. It really must
suck to be our friend right now. Russia has stated that for
the first time they are equals in the negotiations. I think
maybe they are understating a bit. They have the upper
hand. These two stories today show a clear path towards
our disarmament while our enemies keep building
arsenals. And since we have stated flatly that we are not
going to retaliate forcefully to an attack, it is just a matter

76

of time. Sure seems a lot like giving comfort to an enemy. What do you call it when a president intentionally jeopardizes national security? I call it treason.
April 6 at 9:28am

Tim Kirby - *I forgot to mention that there is a provision allowing Russian to opt out later. It doesn't take much to see who is pulling the strings. Reagan is turning over in his grave. We win the cold war and then give our old enemy the keys to the store. God we need another Joe McCarthy right about now.*
April 6 at 9:35am

Lisa Hoag - GREAT! I will keep my mouth shut since I'm NOT in the mood now to listen to excuses and apologies for the "MAN" in office. WTF....I take it by no responses maybe even the left doesn't know wtf he is doing this time!!!
April 6 at 11:43am

Tim Kirby - I am sure the left knows they just don't care. A lot of my posts don't get replies. People read, absorb the info and move on. Replies only happen when the left feels strongly that I am wrong. This item is incontrovertible.
April 6 at 12:38pm

Penny Hanson - This to me is so very scary....
April 6 at 4:12pm

Michael Tipsword - Not good. Considering Russia's relationship with Iran, we should be VERY wary. And, of course, Putin isn't to be trusted in any way.
April 6 at 5:47pm

Lisa Hoag - Knock me over with a feather.... or should that be butter my biscuit.
April 6 at 5:58pm

April 7, 2010 - NASA

Tim Kirby - *Also today, I found out that, since Obama has decided to cut NASA funding and we are not going to afford to develop a replacement for the shuttle fleet which is scheduled to be grounded this year, we are going to pay Russia $55million per astronaut to hitch rides on Soyuz capsules. Remember back when that paragon of the left, JFK made it a priority to BEAT Russia in the space race?*
April 7 at 2:58pm

Tiffany Atkinson - It almost seems like Obama is trying to dumb down America...we have been known as the best for years and now with this Presidents it seems like he is trying to make us blend in instead of standing out
April 7 at 3:02pm

Tim Kirby - *Obama does not believe in the concept of American Exceptionalism. He is treating foreign policy the same as his domestic socialism. He is ceding everything we as a Nation have fought for to our enemies and turning his back on longtime friends. Reagan described the USSR as the "evil empire" but Obama believes it is America that is evil and we deserve to collapse. Remember, he was taught as a child in a madrasa by Imams who refer to America as*

the "great satan"
Wed at 3:24pm

April 8, 2010 – Qatari Shoe Bomber

Tim Kirby - *An idiot from the Qatar embassy was on a domestic flight last night and decided he needed to go in the bathroom and smoke. Then he thought it would be funny to tell marshals on the plane that he was trying to light his shoes. I guess he has a different sense of humor. Middle easterners threatening to blow up planes, NOT funny.*
April 8 at 7:14am

Terri Collins - Heath Diplomatic immunity is a crock.
April 8 at 8:37am

Tim Kirby - *UPDATE - The chucklehead from Qatar is not going to be charged with anything, not even the smoking, because of diplomatic immunity.*
April 8 at 8:36am

Terri Collins - Heath HA! I refer you to my previous comment. (Diplomatic immunity is a crock!)
April 8 at 8:42am

April 8, 2010 – More START News

Tim Kirby - *UPDATE - Obama signed the Nuclear Reduction treaty with Russia this morning. Now we need the Senate to block it.*
April 8 at 8:38am

Doug Maddox - I'm not surprised that Obama is so soft on defense...typical Democratic President
April 8 at 9:01am

April 9, 2010 – Stupak Quits

Tim Kirby - *We had a little good news today, for a change. Bart Stupak announced he will retire at the end of his term. Too bad he didn't quit before tossing out his beliefs*
April 9 at 1:07pm

Michael Tipsword - He didn't do a good enough job of explaining his choice to support HR 3200 in light of his Anti-Abortion Rights stance. Do I have the source of contention correct?
April 9 at 2:19pm

Doug Maddox - He supported life in his campaign, but did not do so in his vote.
April 9 at 2:23pm

Tim Kirby - *Yep.*
April 9 at 2:56pm

April 9, 2010 – Opening in the Supremes

Tim Kirby - *Bad news. With Souter retiring Obama can appoint another Soto Mayor.*
April 9 at 1:08pm

Tim Kirby - *Oops, I misspoke. Stevens is retiring, not Souter. I had Souter on my mind when I posted that. Sorry.*
April 9 at 1:15pm

Michael Tipsword - Hopefully they can find someone as good at uniting the Supreme Court regardless of political ideology. I'd support the appointment of another world-wise and experienced minority. The SC has been ruled by rich old white people for far too long.
April 9 at 2:17pm

Tim Kirby - *As good as who? Stevens or Soto Mayor? Neither is good. They are both activist justices who want to put their stamp on history by violating the separation of powers and attempting to create law. What is needed is a strict constructionist who will actually enforce the constitution.*
April 9 at 2:55pm

Single Status Updates Without Comments

Referencing The Socialist turn in Americas Direction

Tim Kirby - *Chris Mathews calls West Point the "enemy camp" on MSNBC last night. Isn't that getting real close to treason?*
December 2, 2009 at 12:53pm

Tim Kirby - *American has been teetering on the edge of an abyss for a year now, and tonight we finally took that step over the edge and are falling headfirst into Socialism*
March 21 at 10:22pm

Tim Kirby - *Welcome to "The People's Republic of America"*
March 21 at 10:23pm

Tim Kirby - *The last time the people of this country were this divided, an overzealous President had Federal troops open fire on Ft. Sumter.*
March 21 at 10:38pm

Tim Kirby - *Nov 2, 2010*
March 21 at 10:39pm

Tim Kirby - *This might be a good time to move to Texas. I'll bet them crazy cowboys try to secede.*
March 21 at 10:46pm

Tim Kirby - *Since it looks like all us taxpayers will now be finding abortions, maybe we can fun someway to remove the president and it can be an "O-bortion"*
March 21 at 10:58pm

Tim Kirby - *I am going to start searching the internet for Confederate money. I got a feeling it is going to have value*

again soon.
March 22 at 9:48am

Tim Kirby - *People die every day in their sleep. No noise, no convulsions, just a last gasp of breath and they are gone. Such we have witnessed in the passing of Liberty, as we all painfully listened to the sound of the plug as it was pulled.*
March 22 at 11:33pm

Tim Kirby - *Everyone on the left has been making a big deal about the actions of certain members of the Tea Bag movement, it goes both ways! Here is a headline. "Ann Coulter Ottawa speech shut down... 2000 protesters surrounding building with rocks and sticks -- pulled fire alarm in building. Cops shut it down! Blogs calling for Coulter to be hurt. MPs were banned from going, Coulter denounced by an MP in the Parliament."*
March 23 at 9:14pm

Tim Kirby - *I think this headline speaks for itself. And it speaks volumes. "REVOLUTION: CASTRO CHEERS OBAMACARE!"*
March 25 at 6:34pm

Tim Kirby - *In case anyone was wondering, yep, I am back on my soapbox tonight. I am locked down in the bunker and listening for the sound of the jackbooted thugs from the Obama secret police knocking on my door. ;-)*
March 25 at 7:17pm

Tim Kirby - *New deal with Russia. Obama vows to cut long range nuclear weapons by a third. So much for national*

85

security. *This disgrace is throwing us all under a RED bus.*
March 26 at 10:50am

Tim Kirby - *I am going to take a well-deserved break tonight to spend some time with Dino since he returned from Florida today. Thanks to all of you who actually read my ramblings and I promise to have more from the Bunker tomorrow. Breaking news as it happens.* До свидания товарищ.
March 26 at 9:51pm

Tim Kirby - *French Economist Frederic Bastiat, on Socialism*

"It is impossible to introduce into society a greater change and a greater evil than this: the conversion of the law into an instrument of plunder…. But how is this legal plunder to be identified? Quite simply. See if the law takes from some persons what belongs to them, and gives it to other persons to whom it does not belong. See if the law benefits one citizen at the expense of another by doing what the citizen himself cannot do without committing a crime."
March 27 at 8:28am

Tim Kirby - *American Economist Walter Williams, on Socialism*

"Can a moral case be made for taking the rightful property of one American and giving it to another to whom it does not belong? I think not. That's why socialism is evil. It uses evil means (coercion) to achieve what are seen as good ends (helping people). We might also note that an act that is inherently evil does not become moral

simply because there's a majority consensus..... For the Christians among us, socialism and the welfare state must be seen as sinful. When God gave Moses the commandment "Thou shalt not steal", I'm sure He didn't mean thou shalt not steal unless there's a majority vote. And, I'm sure that if you asked God if it's okay just being a recipient of stolen property, He would deem that a sin as well."

March 27 at 8:30am

Tim Kirby - *Before any of my worthy opponents on the left flame me, I am aware that I stole "humble narrator" from A Clock Work Orange. I just like the way it sounds, besides, imitation is the sincerest flattery right? Besides, it's not stealing if you give credit.*

March 31 at 12:28pm

Tim Kirby - *Rep. Phil Hare, D-IL, "I don't care about the Constitution"*

At town hall someone started to ask about the constitutionality of the Health Care bill, Rep Hare cut them off and said "I don't care about the Constitution on this. I care more about the people that are dying every day that don't have health insurance". Someone responded "You care more about that than the Constitution you swore to uphold", to which Rep Hare replied that it says "we have a right to life, liberty and the pursuit of happiness." At this point someone corrected him and explained that that was the Declaration of Independence. Rep Hare then said "either one, it doesn't matter to me." When the person asking the question finally pinned him down with the

question "Where in the constitution does it give you the authority.." Rep Hare cuts him off and says "I don't know." Later in the exchange when asked if he was an expert on the topic he could only reply "no, I'm the dreamer." Then he claimed that he read the entire bill three times. When it was explained to him that that was a total of 8100 pages and that at 1 min per page it would take over 5 days of continuous reading he interrupted and asked if they were calling him a liar. The person asking the questions replied "yes" and Rep. Hare left the room.
April 2 at 4:26pm

Tim Kirby - *Gallup first started the approval poll in 1938. In that time, Obama has the lowest approval rating after one year of any other president. Here they are for you to compare. These numbers are as of December. One year after each was elected. In order of popularity*
George W. Bush - 86% (How about that?)
John F. Kennedy - 77%
Lyndon B. Johnson - 74% (this was before the war ramped up)
George H. W. Bush - 71%
Dwight D. Eisenhower - 69% (America loves it's war heroes)
Richard M. Nixon - 59%
Jimmy Carter - 57%
Gerald Ford - 52%
William J. Clinton - 52%
Harry S Truman - 49%
Ronald W. Reagan - 49%
Barack H. Obama - 47%
April 2 at 4:52pm

Tim Kirby - *Has anyone else noticed that Obama's speeches are sounding less like a sitting president talking about policy and more like campaign speeches? Lots of sound bites, some shouting like a tent revival, and very little substance.*
April 5 at 8:18am

Tim Kirby - *I read over the weekend about a tea party rally in Nevada last month. Some eggs were thrown and a man in the crowd immediately told a police officer that tea partiers were throwing the eggs at him and some other folks that came out to oppose the rally. The gentleman was a Dem party official in NV. Problem is, Brietbart had his cameras rolling and this guy was the one that threw the eggs to discredit the tea party.*

I guess just accusing without substantiation like in DC on vote day last month are not enough since that tactic didn't work. Now they have to plant operatives with in the rallies to stir dissention and discredit the tea party. These people are really running scared.
April 5 at 10:43am

Tim Kirby - *According to the Mayans it's all over in Dec. 2012, I just hope we last that long. Because at this point it is not looking good for the USA. 3 more years of Obama is going to be hard for the Nation to endure. In one year he has done more damage that the other 43 Presidents combined. Just realized Dec. 2012 would be one month after Obama's re-election if it were to happen. Maybe those Mayans did know something??*
April 6 at 6:38am

89

Tim Kirby - *Our fearless leader does it again. After he threw out the first pitch at the Nationals home opener(he throws like a girl) he was interviewed in the booth about his Sox hat. He made a big deal about the Southside. When asked who his favorite player was back in the day, he couldn't name a single player. He also referred to growing up near "Kaminski" park. Don't sound like no Chi boy to me.*
April 6 at 4:34pm

Tim Kirby - *I would love to wake up one morning and have nothing to post. BUT, the White House is revamping the National Security Strategy to remove offensive terms like "Islamic radicalism". The last time I check, that was the greatest threat to our security. Remember 9/11 Barack?*

He says he converted from Islam to Christianity, but he hasn't attended church since moving to Washington, and he continues kowtowing to Muslin leaders. I think we are seeing where his allegiance is really at.
April 7 at 6:24am

Tim Kirby - *And this is how our BIGGEST threat (a Muslim nation) feels about our President, "Mr. Obama, you are a newcomer (to politics). Wait until your sweat dries and get some experience. Be careful not to read just any paper put in front of you or repeat any statement recommended,(American officials) bigger than you, more bullying than you, couldn't do a damn thing, let alone you." - Ahmadinejad*

It is so nice to know that Obama has done such a good job making the world love him, that a nutjob like

Ahmadinejad has absolutely no respect
April 7 at 6:28am

Tim Kirby - *A senior Chinese diplomat has said that after a call between Obama and Hu, China and America have reached "a new consensus." Tianaka says this is because of a "fresh approach" by Obama on Tibet and Taiwan. I have been saying all week, it must really suck to be our friend now, but our enemies are living large.*
April 7 at 2:55pm

Tim Kirby - *It is getting to the point that I don't even like to get up in the morning for fear of what the news will bring. Today I give you this quote, "If America presents Iran with a serious threat and undertakes any measure against Iran, none of the American soldiers who are currently in the region would go back to America alive," Major General Hassan Firouzabadi of Iran.*

I REALLY miss the days when we were in a position of strength. Have you noticed that Iran on gets belligerent when there is a Dem in the White House who is soft on defense, think Jimmy Carter and the hostages.
Thu at 6:35am

Tim Kirby - *To B. Netanyahu. Mr. Prime Minister remember the words of Pat Buchanan, "It is dangerous to be America's enemy, but fatal to be America's friend". I am sorry, for the treatment the Obama regime has given you. There are still some here that support Israel.*
Yesterday at 6:12pm

Wesley Cramer's Thread

Wesley Cramer - "Associate with men of good quality if you esteem your own reputation; for it is better to be alone than in bad company." George Washington.
March 27 at 5:20am

Wesley Cramer - Hannity tried to warn us. Beck has documented. Watch with who people surround themselves as it is a reflection of what's inside. BHO can't hide behind the generic campaign rhetoric of a centrist.
March 27 at 5:22am

Bob Brown - But Wesley they manipulate everything and tell half of the stories. I listen to them every day at work these so call tea parties are causing violence Hannity and Rush are provoking it. Remember evil begets evil
March 27 at 5:34am

Wesley Cramer -No one cited above encourages violence. Those that say they do, do not listen. The context is completely lost upon the "Rush Limbaugh said" crowd, because that crowd does not listen and does not understand the context and after the first person says "RL said".... they all rabbit it as the truth.

I would also, without reservation, observe that in my lifetime, the most violent demonstrations I have seen are not by those seeking to retain freedom and liberty, but rather those that seek to limit choices, freedom, democracy and destroy capitalism. Demonstrations at the G-XX (pick a number) meetings come to mind.
March 27 at 5:52am

Bob Brown - First let me say i am not demo or repub i am just a bi stander so why are all these democrats offices getting vandalized and are also getting death threats. people are being told to protest in front of their houses because of this health bill grant it i don't agree or understand the bill but something has to be done. If these "tea baggers" don't calm down all its going to cause is riots. March 27 at 6:20am

Wesley Cramer - The right to peacefully assemble and free speech mostly still exists today, but apparently more so for the left than the right in the main stream media's eyes.

To seek redress, it is incumbent upon one to speak. I have yet to hear a single person advocate a violent act or to condone one. In any assembly of persons, there will be a variety of personalities. So some are prone to be more reserved and others more radical. It is a simple fact.

It is assumed that those that love liberty are responsible for the acts of intimidation you cite. Maybe, maybe not. It could just as easily be lefties playing a chess game knowing the end result will be more restrictions against basic freedoms of Americans. I am suspicious of all in political arena, of those that hold the power to tax and regulate and I am equally wary of those who disseminate information regarding the same. The violence noted may be from the right, the left, or someone just looking for an excuse. Who knows at this point?

It is a sad statement that the media, the left media, has attempted to vilify and stigmatize the notion of a "tea party" and its participants. Is it no wonder they use a sex act to degrade and marginalize them? It clearly portrays contempt. It is yet another way to disassociate Americans with their history, and another way to change the paradigm of the discussion so that truth is without relevance in the discussion and eventually lost.

The fear of riots is perpetuated by the left to shut the right up.

Parenthetically, of course riots against the right is people harmlessly exercising their freedom and seeking redress for the wrongs of the world and evil capitalism...
March 27 at 6:16am

Wesley Cramer - BTW Bob, while I gave credit to Hannity and Beck in my original comment, I will state for the record that I don't completely agree with everything they state, nor do I think they are completely accurate in their representations.

Each of us has to sniff out the truth. If in doubt, err to the side of caution. Saying 'no' is not permanent and an easily rectified mistake. Saying yes nearly always is permanent. Infinitely more mistakes are made by saying yes than saying no.

I will also state that they, along with a scant few others, shed more light on the fullness of an issue than any one at any other major news source. Two words to demonstrate the wholeness of this conversation.... "Van Jones"
March 27 at 7:24am

Tim Kirby - *Can I get in on this? I just wanted to add that the only REAL violence that has been committed since HC passed was against a Republican. A shot was fired through the window of House Minority Whip Eric Cantor's office.*

96

As far as the "violence" against the left, this is being blown out of proportion by the state run media outlets such as CNN and Pravda, sorry I meant to say MSNBC, an easy mistake. The Dems are trying to use these "attacks" as campaign items. One of General Secretary Obama's own campaign people was out campaigning for a Dem member of the House use the "violence" to try to drum up support. And Obama himself has been using inflammatory and derogatory language in his speeches as well.

Also let's not forget that the Tea Party movement took their name from a group practicing civil disobedience 230 years ago. I do not advocate violence, but I do think we are headed towards the 2nd American Civil War, or perhaps it would be better called the 2nd War for Independence. We already have a group of military officers called the "Oath Keepers" who have sworn to uphold the constitution regardless of what orders they get from the "Commander in Chief".

Remember also, the framers included the 2nd amendment precisely so that we would be able to protect our self should the limited government the created every become tyrannical.

I should also state that while I do listen to Rush and Hannity occasionally, I get most of my news and

information from other sources. And I think Glenn Beck is a little out there and do not listen to him. He is our sides Olbermann. IMHO
March 27 at 8:05 am

Sharon Weyrick Harris - Well said Wes and Tim!!! I second that. All the votes that were 'bought' last week have been

promised a deal. Most of them will end up with an appointed position on this administration's staff after they lose their office in the next election.
March 27 at 8:24am

Bob Brown - I agree maybe i have been misled i guess i should stay out of it i know enough about politics to fill a thimble lol. I just go by what's on the radio it's so hard to figure out who is right when all sides think they are right. Heck Wesley you're probably right.
March 27 at 11:09am

Tim Kirby - *Bob, do NOT "stay out of it." IT is your right and obligation as an American to be involved. Simply educate yourself on the issues. You have already taken the first steps by just getting involved in online debates. Keep it up.*
March 27 at 11:12am

Bob Brown - ok will do! Be back later
March 27 at 11:15am

Wesley Cramer - Yupper Bob. Everyone needs to keep involved, even though it does wear on ya from time to time...
March 27 at 1:07pm

Natalie Hillary-Fluhr - Well said everyone. Bob don't just give up. Hang in there and learn what the truth is and that can be hard sometimes because we have integrity and truth in all media (TV, radio, print). Everyone seems to have a political agenda instead of the truth. We are all better off if we listen to both sides and then reason and think for ourselves and figure out the truth. There will always be people on the right and on the left and then those that are just psychos out there that want to rebel or cause violence. The media must remember just because one person does violence does not mean that the rest of the group does. We all must remember also to educate ourselves in the history of the founding principles we based on. We were not founded by republicans or democrats but on people seeking liberty and freedom from a tyrannical government. They did not want no government or big government they wanted limited government and that is what we should try to lean towards also. I am not a republican or democrat, have never been. I try to research and figure out what the candidate really stands for and then base my vote on that. There is a reason our founders said to elect men of upstanding character. Character does matter!

March 27 at 3:51pm

Tina Gooch's Obama Thread

Tina Gooch - So tired of listening to EVERYONE bitch about how crappy a President, Obama, is!! It is amazing how it took 8 years to screw up this nation but Obama should be a miracle worker and fix it in 1!! I encourage everyone that bitches about it all the time to write a letter to the President and tell him what he should be doing to "FIX" everything in a year since it is quite apparent they have better degrees than he has!
December 17, 2009 at 9:17am

Tracy L. Smith - I second that! Just think of where we'd be if McCain/Palin were in office now. That's scary!!!
December 17, 2009 at 9:24am

Vincent Post - You tell them Tina, Republicans suck!!!Especially one's named BUSH!!!!!!!
December 17, 2009 at 9:44am

Jeff Miller - I agree that Bush is retarded and lied to all of us. However I do not agree with the Cap n trade. Which will drive up production costs therefore sending businesses out of the U.S. Creating more unemployment
December 17, 2009 at 10:03am

Quinnette Rose Mullins - I third that!! I get so sick of people who think they have such great ideas to fix things. If they were so damn great, they wouldn't be on FB bitching about it, they would be at the white house taking care of it! People crack me up when they blame Obama. He is not a miracle worker; it was Bush that got us into this mess! Obama just got stuck with the mess to clean up!
December 17, 2009 at 10:05am

102

Jeff Miller, I understand that it's not gonna get fixed overnight. Probably won't be fixed in 4 yrs.
December 17, 2009 at 10:14am

Emily Bledsoe - Uhmmmmmmm.. It wasn't Bush that led us to where we were. It was Clinton, he was to finish what the 1st Bush started & instead opted for head & cigars!
December 17, 2009 at 11:14am

Jeff Miller - Both Bushes and Clinton lied to us
    3 presidents in a row ALL LIARS. And what's wrong with a BJ? Nothing
December 17, 2009 at 11:18am

Emily Bledsoe - Ha-ha.. Okay, I'll give ya that, Jeff :)
December 17, 2009 at 11:21am

Jeff Miller - I agree 100 % Rusty
December 17, 2009 at 11:46am

Tina Gooch - Okay so what do we do with that????
December 17, 2009 at 12:28pm

Jeff Miller - We sit back and watch and pray and hope that our leader makes the right choices
December 17, 2009 at 12:33pm

Tina Gooch - I say we just stop voting....doesn't matter what they say before we vote them in, it all changes once they get in office. And I am not just talking about the President. LOL
December 17, 2009 at 12:38pm

103

Jeff Miller - Well. You have a valid point

December 17, 2009 at 12:50pm

Rory Monique Smith – I've got it!!! I can let him borrow the magic wand that apparently some doctors think I have to use when their patients are FUBAR!!! ;)

December 17, 2009 at 1:01pm

Jeff Miller - Rory...you watch too many Cheesy movies...Tango & cash

December 17, 2009 at 1:11pm

Tim Kirby - *The problem in not that Obama "didn't fix it", it is that he has made things much worse in a year. He has run up the deficit 3x higher in one year that Bush did in 8. He is spending money faster than any president in history. He has moved the government farther into the private sector than ever before by taking over the auto and banking industries. He is trying to do the same thing with the health care industry now. He has made concessions to terrorists and their sponsor nations and traveled the globe "apologizing". He is bringing enemy combatants into this country to stand trial and giving them the rights of American citizens. These trials will destroy the intelligence community and do irreparable harm to our national security. He has turned his back on our longtime ally Israel. Like you said, all of this is just in one year. I don't think we can withstand 7 more. I don't want the President to "fix" anything. I just want him to get out of my life and to take congress with him.*

December 17, 2009 at 2:30pm

Tim Kirby - *As far as "degrees" Obama is not a noted scholar. And he has absolutely no real world experience. Being a community activist is a long way from having a real job and understanding the people. He is an elitist who just thinks that he is better than the people he serves.*
December 17, 2009 at 2:32pm

Tim Kirby - *one last note, I'm not a big Bush supporter either, so don't start attacking me with that. I am a CONSERVATIVE and we haven't had one of those since Reagan and look at the prosperity we had then. I think everyone will agree that the 80's were a great time to be an American.*
December 17, 2009 at 2:34pm

Tina Gooch - He hasn't run the deficit up as high as you think. The official deficit number for FY2008 was around $480billion but was actually $10.6trillion because Bush declined to account for the war and TARP which Obama ended and included them in the budget. So he has NOT run the deficit as high as you think. A lot of the money that he has loaned to the banks is being returned a little at a time which helped the economy regardless of what you may think at least the banks did not close and a lot of people kept their jobs. It wasn't President Obama that allowed the banks to loan money to people that couldn't afford the payments! If anyone's interested in exploring global debt further, and how it's changed over time, check out the Economist's new Global Debt Clock, here:
<link removed>
December 17, 2009 at 3:08pm

105

Tina Gooch - OH... one thing i have learned in the last few years... ALL Bush supporters became CONSERVATIVE!!!!
December 17, 2009 at 3:09pm

Tina Gooch - As far as him being a scholar, please do research prior to making comments!!!!....Barack Obama attended Occidental College, but received his undergraduate degree in political science from Columbia University, an Ivy League member currently ranked 9th in the country by U.S. News and World Report. Obama also graduated Magna Cum Laude from the Harvard Law School, where he also served as President of the Harvard Law Review. Harvard Law School is ranked the best Law School in America.

Columbia University - B.A. political science with a specialization in international relations.

Harvard - Juris Doctor (J.D.) Magna Cum Laude
December 17, 2009 at 3:12pm

Tim Kirby - *A. I did know Obama's education. I did not need to Google his bio and copy/paste it into my post.*

B. a PoliSci degree does not make one scholarly nor does a law degree so I stand by that comment.

C. Bush was NOT a conservative so maybe it is you who should research facts.

D. At no point during the last 8 years did I support Bush's fiscal policy with the exception of tax cuts.

E. I have noticed that it is the left that resorts to making personal attacks when they can't win on the issues.
December 17, 2009 at 3:55pm

106

Tim Kirby - *One last thing, Bush is gone; he is not coming back so it is time for the left to let go of the past. Although 44% of Americans do want him back.*

December 17, 2009 at 4:02pm

Kim S Coon - Heck this was educational reading and well worth it. Thanks Tina for the post that got everyone weighing in. Tim you amaze me at times. You are a very smart person, not that I did not think you were stupid just did not know the depth. Wow

December 17, 2009 at 4:33pm

Vincent Post - what in the world would you want Bush back for, target practice? as for Reagan didn't they catch a couple of his boys bringing loads of cocaine into the country while Nancy and him go to all the schools to tell the kids just say NO !!!!

December 17, 2009 at 5:37pm

Tim Kirby - *I didn't say I wanted Bush back. I said a recent poll showed 44% would prefer to have him back over the current situation. That is huge when you realize he left office with approval ratings in the teens. By implying that I said I wanted him back is a typical example of the leftist tactic of misquoting. Also, implying a Reagan/coke connection is not only absurd but also even a little too tasteless for the left. If you doubt what Reagan did for this country I would recommend reading the declassified KGB files on him. As far as the target practice comment, it is things like that which totally discredit the lefts position, so carry on.*

December 17, 2009 at 5:56pm

Manuela Schabel - Tina...if you wanted this much attention, why didn't you just call me...I wanted have taken you "out on the town"!!! Btw...you forget the Democrats are starting to NOT SIDE with our President, along with many of those who voted for him last year!!!
December 17, 2009 at 6:04pm

Manuela Schabel - And let me stir the pot some more...we have elected a "rock star", not a President!
December 17, 2009 at 6:05pm

Jeff Miller - Let's all hug n kiss. No need for fighting
December 17, 2009 at 6:08pm

Manuela Schabel - LOL...Jeff...Tina knows I'm a "lover", not a "fighter".
December 17, 2009 at 6:09pm

Jeff Miller - I'm a hell of a fighter but sure do like the Lovin'. Hehehehe
December 17, 2009 at 6:15pm

Nicole Marie Lawson - Mom.. quit trying to start a debate.. I don't know this Tim Kirby guy but i think I am going to have to agree with some of his arguments... I am absolutely pissed about your "wonderful" Obama sending over more troops. What happened to blowing there damn country up and coming back home?? Instead we give them time to kill our troops, we rebuild their cities and still help support there elections.. how ridiculous is that?? Yet they did not bring their asses here to clean our mess of 9-11. Obama is

or ANTI-CHRIST!! lol ... u will see
December 18, 2009 at 7:49am

Tina Gooch – My, my, my...........just look what I miss when I don't get on here at night...LOL.... This has been a great conversation if I should say so myself.... wonder what my next status update will be...he he.... Jeff.... thanks for your input, kept it going... Tim... it is nice to see that you are passionate about something other than depressing posts... thanks for your input too, it has been a pleasure seeing your posts... Manny... I will take care of you later...lmao...up for pickle shots???..... Vinnie you are awesome as usual.... Nicole you are not even dry behind the ears yet so your input doesn't count...love you all!!!!
December 18, 2009 at 8:31am

Lisa Hoag's Thread on Health Care

Lisa Hoag - I have to stop vacationing! At least one of two things are certain to happen, I will get sick or our country continues to take another step into socialism...I was on vac. when Obama was elected and now as he ruins our health care!
March 22 at 10:57am

Lisa Hoag - Oh wait! I won't have to worry about it...once this bill goes into effect I WONT BE ABLE TO AFFORD A VACATION!!!
March 22 at 11:00am

Larry Lee - OMG Lisa!! People making over 200k a year are the only ones who will see an increase in their taxes which amounts to an extra $400.00 a year. I think they can afford it! Your taxes are paying for universal health care in Iraq. That's right. GWB allocated 13 billion dollars to Iraq to give them universal health care 5 years ago. Almost everything we get and take for granted is a social program of some sort. This bill is actually LESS of a social program. People have seriously got to look at what the bill actually does instead of listening to talking points.
March 22 at 11:40am

Kevin Polson - Lisa....from now on, you have to work for the rest of your life...or just until we have a responsible individual back in office...preferably a Republican. ;-)
March 22 at 11:47am

Tim Kirby - *EVERYBODY is going to suffer with this! Since it is unconstitutional maybe the court will strike it down.*

Welcome to the People's Republic of American.
March 22 at 11:55am

Lisa Hoag - Larry the bad part is that the way we file taxes being farmers it looks like we make more than 400K a year even though that isn't what we bring home clear. They don't care that we have to pay for all the seeds, fert, weed control etc... Kevin being farmers we are sooo Republicans. You have to be to watch out for your interests even though they are not as profitable as the fat cat business men it ends up treating us like them!!
March 22 at 12:20pm

Lisa Hoag - I also would like to point out that $400 can mean the difference between vacation or not when you have 2 kids in college one going to a state school at 26K or more a year. Every penny counts to us too!
March 22 at 12:22pm

Larry Lee - Lisa, true as farmers you get screwed the worst!
The last administration was responsible with spending? LMFAO!
Republicans & Democrats both think they are the responsible ones when it comes to spending. I am pointing out that everyone should have figured put by now that NEITHER party benefits you no matter which party you support. In case you have not noticed I am Independent and think both parties are full of Sh*t!
March 22 at 12:34pm

Brian Cooper - RELIGION anyone?
March 22 at 1:04pm

113

Larry Lee - LOL@ Brian! ;-)
March 22 at 1:08pm

Lisa Hoag - Brian....LOL!
March 22 at 2:21pm

Todd Lawson -Larry now if the heath care flops I'm sure the democrats will blame it on GWB or the republicans like they always do even though when GWB was in office the democrats had the majority of the vote. But everyone seems to forget that, right!
March 22 at 4:52pm

Larry Lee - Obviously you forget they only had the majority for the last 2 years of GWB. All of GWB'S legislation was already pushed through by then. Both parties are hypocrites! When the other is not in power they always say we didn't do it that way. Bullshit! Neither part works for us! They work for themselves. They look out for their own interests and that of the lobbyists.
March 22 at 5:30pm

Todd Lawson -I will agree with you on that, they are not working for us they are working for themselves.
March 22 at 5:31pm

Tim Kirby - *That stat is kind of misleading Larry. The Republicans never had a filibuster proof majority in the senate during the Bush years. And unlike the current Dems, the GOP never got creative with the rules to circumvent the filibuster, even when the Dems were doing*

unprecedented things like filibustering judicial nominees.
March 22 at 6:04pm

Tim Kirby - Jeez, how many times can I say filibuster in one post?
March 22 at 6:05pm

Brian Cooper - Once again, anyone wanna talk religion?
March 22 at 6:12pm

Larry Lee - Tim, you really need to check your facts on exactly how that congress operated. They passed many items with a simple majority. They never had a filibuster proof majority. Again, everyone thinks their party does nothing wrong. I will call both political parties on their bullshit any day.
Very Independently Yours. Larry.
March 22 at 6:20pm

Dawn Young - NOW LISA!!! AS A CHRISTIAN, YOU ARE SUPPOSED TO PRAY FOR OUR PRESIDENT NO MATTER WHO HE IS!!HELP HIM ALONG IS THE SECRET!! GOD IS HERE FOR US. LOL, DO I SOUND LIKE A MINISTER, DONT MEAN TO. THIS IS WHY I DONT LIKE GETTING DEEP INTEREST INTO POLITICS CAUSE IT WILL MAKE YOU MAD ALL THE TIME AND THATS NO WAY TO SPEND YOUR LIFE. DONT WORRY BE HAPPY!! LUV YA SIS.
March 22 at 6:29pm

Tim Kirby - *@Larry, I wasn't trying to pick a fight. :-) Just pointing out that they never used shenanigans like we saw this week to get around the filibuster. Sure, many things* *went through the Senate with a simple majority. That is the way it normally works. But the Senate rules allow for the filibuster and it takes 60 votes to get cloture and move on to the actual vote on the bill, which then requires the simple majority to pass. The Democrats DID filibuster sever bills and appointments (the appointments were unprecedented) and the Republican leadership never tried to side step the rules on cloture by using the reconciliation process, which is actually only supposed to be used on budget bills. That was all I was getting at.*

@Brian, you don't want me to the religion route. Since I founded my own religion, Timism, I find that people don't really like discussing it with me.

Rev. Dr. Tim Kirby

Julie Mullen – Lisa, as opposed to CAPITALISM come on Lisa if i got cancer or you got cancer do we both deserve the same health care or do i deserve to die cause right now i don't have a job? Come on I love ya Lisa ENJOY LIFE AND STOP Bitchin like your buddy RUSH LIMBAUGH love your hubby and kids I Love you talk to you later and be safe driving home ok love to you all!!!!
March 22 at 8:57pm

Tim Kirby - *Julie, no one is saying you should not get treatment if you get cancer. But, and this is going to sound bad so I apologize, why should I be expected to pay for it? The entire concept of "spreading wealth" is bullshit. It is nothing more than stealing from someone who earned and giving to someone who didn't.*
March 22 at 9:20pm

116

Dawn Young - Bush's evil ass was no better!!!!! It's not even the president at fault it's the people surrounding him, hello!!!!!
March 22 at 9:45pm

Julie Mullen - I agree with you dawn!!!! Bush was and is NO BETTER!!!! Bush and Dick what a pair!!!!!! They got us into all this crapola
March 22 at 9:57pm

Tim Kirby - *Oh please, the Bush bashing is getting passé. I was not a fan but it is time for the wacky left to move on. He has been out of office for over a year. The use of the word "evil" is simply ridiculous and just makes a joke out of any argument put forth. Limbaugh is evil, beck is evil, Bush is evil, give me a break. And please feel free to continue making Bush and Dick jokes. It only serves to show how immature the left is. As for it not being the president but the people around him, that is laughable. Obama has been pushing this obscene expansion of government power since before the election. Obama wants a socialist America and is well on his way. The abuse of power that was represented with the HC bill is unprecedented in the history of the country. Welcome to "The People's Republic of America" led by General Secretary Obama. It's a joke now, but let's see what happens in the next couple of years.*
March 22 at 10:12pm

Dawn Young - ONLY LISA WOULD START A CONFLICTING PAGE LIKE THIS!!! U KNOW SHE IS LAFIN HER ASS OFF!!!!!YES IM WRITING LIKE I TEXT BECAUSE I DONT GIV A

117

DAM!!NOW!! OBAMA IS ONLY HUMAN JUST LIKE ALL THE OTHERS WHO MADE BIG MISTAKES IN OFFICE!!!!!JUST CAUSE HE HES COOL CALM AND COLLECTIVE DOESNT MEAN HE CAN FIX LIFE LONG PROBLEMS IN 1 YR!!! LOL!!!OK LET ME STOP!
March 22 at 10:27pm

Julie Mullen - Dawn again I would have to agree with ya. Bush is suicidal and Dick can't recall it is kinda funny ya know and Tim the wacky left come on and WHO said YOU would PAY FOR MY CANCER TREATMENTS!!! If we all ate better fruits and vegetables as opposed to FAST FOOD and GETTING FAT we wouldn't have all this crap going on so you can take your red all the way to the right crap and shove it!!!
March 23 at 2:28am

Tim Kirby - *If YOU are getting free health care WHO do YOU think is paying for it? Hint, those of us with a job. Where do you think the money comes from, the health care fairy? It comes out of my and everyone else with a job's taxes. Anytime you get something for nothing someone else had to pay for it. And for the last time Bush and Cheney are gone and they won't be back. Get over it and GROW UP. And Dawn, I don't care if Obama is cool, calm, and COLLECTED, he is a Socialist, a threat to this country, our way of life, and a douche. He and his cronies Pelosi and Reid wiped their ass with the constitution on Sunday and anyone who doesn't see that is either blind, naive, in denial, or just as big a douche as he is.*
March 23 at 4:13am

Beverly Gardner-Schwab - I agree with you Tim
March 23 at 4:46pm

Julie Mullen - Well Tim I think you are a big douche bag yourself a threat to the country come on what choice did we have old man and Bush in a skirt or Obama come on you are a jerk!!!!
March 23 at 7:43pm

Tim Kirby - *Typical tactic of the lunatic left. When you can't win a debate on issues resort to name calling. Maybe if you did your homework Julie you could actually have an intellectual discussion instead of childishness. I realize I am asking a lot of someone on the left, wanting you to act like an adult instead of an elementary school child. So I am a douchebag and a jerk because I am more educated than you? Fair enough. I don't understand why you can't let the Bush thing go. He has been out of office for over a year. He is not eligible to run again so GET OVER IT. You don't hear me whining about Jimmy Carter. As far as McCain, yea he is old. He also has experience in global politics. What was Obama? Oh yeah a community organizer. What the hell does that even mean? I am sorry that I don't want my taxes to go towards supporting others. I work my ass off to support my family and don't want more of my money taken away to give to leeches looking for a hand out. Before you even start, there ARE jobs out there. Maybe not glamorous, but there is always retail and fast food if some actually wants to support themselves instead of sponging off of society. Obama IS a threat to the American way of life. He is a Socialist and that flies against everything this*

119

country was built on. Even his pal Al Sharpton admitted Obama is a Socialist. We need a man like Joe McCarthy again now more than ever. I realize you have no idea who or what I am talking about, Google it. It is not my responsibility to educate you on stuff you should have learned in school if you had paid attention. I am done dealing with you; you do not have the knowledge needed to even begin to discuss Health Care on a mature level so I am not going to try. Feel free to call me all the names you like in your next post, it just makes YOU look bad, not me.
March 23 at 8:17pm

Tim Kirby - *I almost forgot NA NA NA NA NA NAAAAA*
March 23 at 8:17pm

Brian Cooper - Religion anyone? C'mon it's fun too.
March 24 at 4:40pm

Britny Hoag - lmao. ha-ha i agree with you Brian, but i don't think we wanna see another 984509234 comments on a post all over our home page again.

As for you Timothy and Julie.. I think you both are acting childish and taking a post (that LISA (aka. mom) should not have posted in the first place) too far. Whether you're on the left or right side, for Obama or against, HATE Bush or love him, it is what it is and you two fighting or having a pissing contest over who's right and who's wrong about their beliefs isn't going to make the economy, the public, or even the president ANY better. Just accept the fact you both have different opinions, anddd that MEANSSS neither of you are right OR wrong.

..That was my good deed for the day :)
March 24 at 8:39pm

Brian Cooper - You go Hottie, I hope LISA reads that
comment.. GO BRIT
March 24 at 8:47pm

Tim Kirby - *Britny, you know I love you, BUT, I was not
being childish. It was not I who lowered myself to name
calling. I was merely stating the FACTS. And YES, there is a
right and a wrong to this. Like I said, you know I love you,
BUT, you are in school, have never had a job, get your
health care through your parents, and have NEVER paid
taxes. When these things change, then we can discuss this
again.*
March 24 at 8:58pm

Lisa Hoag - K Brian's that's about enuff!
March 24 at 9:16pm

**[At this point there was a rather lengthy post from me
about religion. If you have an interest in this I have
included it in an appendix at the end of the book]**

Britny Hoag - First off who cares if I've never had a job, paid
for my own health care, paid taxes, or even voted in a
general election. No i may NOT know every little detail or
understand every little thing.. but ATLEAST I know the
definition of an opinion and that everyone has the right to
their own.. and that in term states that no one has a right
OR wrong opinion. So shut it timothy. Just because I'm not
on top of the hill and on my way back down in age doesn't

make me an idiot. Just as many people would argue your point as they would Julie's. 2nd don't *start* with the religion junk.. it took me 20 minutes to scroll down the page to post this comment, so I'm sure as heck not gonna take another 20 just to read what you said. that = waste of my time. Love you Uncle Timmy :) ha-ha

Brian- ha-ha thanksssss. but you better watch it, or my mom is not gonna allow you within a 20 mile radius of our household lol
March 25 at 10:33pm

Tim Kirby - *Brian has been asking for religion comments for 2 days. I just wanted to give him what he asked for. I wasn't saying that everyone is not entitled to an opinion, just that the opinion of people wanting something for nothing is wrong. And yes there IS a right and wrong answer to this. The right answer is the one that allows me to keep the money I earn. I was also not implying that you were not knowledgeable, just that you need to pay taxes before you can understand why someone who DOES pay taxes is upset.*

I will cut you a little slack because of your age. As they say, "if you are not a liberal when you are young, you are heartless. If you are not a conservative when you are older, you are brainless."
March 25 at 11:24pm

Brian Cooper - Actually, Lisa, Tim, Larry, Brit, and Julie my point is / was I love you guys and to remind you though entitled to your own opinion not to let it get out of control

because the cost may be more than the worth. COOPA
March 26 at 6:02am

Britny Hoag - Yea yea.
March 26 at 10:06am

Lisa Hoag - Dang!!! All I was sayin' is I can't & probably
shouldn't go on anymore vacations! Baaaahaaaa!
March 26 at 3:32pm

Tim Kirby - *Lisa, you know I never said anything you were
not thinking. You just used me as your attack dog.*
March 26 at 3:49pm

Tim Kirby - *Woof!*
March 26 at 3:49pm

Jammin' Jimmy Bean Threads

Oct. 1, 2009 - Chief Illiniwek

Jammin' Jimmy Bean - Hopes not to offend too many but..............If you are in favor of bringing back The Chief are you also in favor of bringing back The Third Reich and bringing back slavery. Do you not understand how offensive this is?
October 1, 2009 at 10:10am

Jason Barham - Do I have to be in favor of the Nazi party and slavery? Because I'm not in favor of either of those, but I do miss seeing Chief Illiniwek at halftime. And I'm not offended - just aware that we probably don't look at that particular issue in the same way.
October 1, 2009 at 10:29am

Tim Kirby - *I have to disagree Jim. As one of both Native American and Jewish decent I think your comparison is flawed. While I agree that the European treatment of Native Americans was deplorable, the Chief is not a reflection of that. The Chief is a celebration of the fighting spirit of the Native Americans. I don't think anyone would say the Chiefs dance is a glorification of genocide. I think a better comparison would be with the Holocaust Museum in Berlin or the King monument in Washington. Besides, the Chief has traditionally been portrayed by a Jewish student.*
October 1, 2009 at 10:44am

Tim Kirby - Also, using your rational, wouldn't the Dallas Cowboys be a more offensive mascot on a par with the

Third Reich?

October 1, 2009 at 10:55am

John Hoeffleur - To claim that people of any ethnicity are monolithic or in general share a characteristic across the board (i.e. "fighting spirit of Native Americans") - whether you mean it to be complementary or not - is not only inaccurate but also the kind of flawed logic that leads to racist attitudes. Just my two cents.

Cowboy is an occupation. No one is born a cowboy. Sub in Notre Dame and you have a point - except that it's a private institution and private institutions are free to defame ethnicities tastelessly if they so choose. Not with my tax money though.

As far as debates goes, it's an oldie but a goodie. Props all around. Thanks gents.

October 1, 2009 at 10:59am

Jammin' Jimmy Bean - I didn't mean to compare, simply to point out we have, hopefully, moved beyond INTENTIONALLY offending people about the wrongs done in the past. Why is it so easy to dismiss the suffering of Native Americans?

October 1, 2009 at 11:05am

Jason Barham - I don't think many, if any, people who support Chief Illiniwek are unaware of the plight of Native Americans today.

October 1, 2009 at 11:08am

Jammin' Jimmy Bean - Great points John! The Illiniwek tribe were farmers not fighters, hence they didn't fare too well

127

when it came time to defend their land. The "Fighting" part of "Fighting Illini" was adopted during W.W.1 to honor alumni, past, present, and future who were serving overseas. Many colleges in America added "Fighting" to their names at that time.
October 1, 2009 at 11:14am

Tim Kirby - *I apologize if I appeared racially insensitive with my generalization. My grandmother was a full blooded Apache. I was actually speaking from a perspective of racial pride. Sorry if it came across wrong. I was purposely being absurd with the cowboy comment to prove a point. That anything can be offensive to someone if you try hard enough. (Not all Germans were Nazis either) As has been said, it's fun to debate but is really kind of moot. I think we all know the Chief is never coming back. Just as an aside, on my mother's side I am Scots-Irish and I don't have a problem with Notre Dame either.*
October 1, 2009 at 11:24am

Phil Strang - While I may agree that the Chief is a "Different" or "special" case and not meant to harm or debase anyone. The fact is he is not a Native American or an accurate depiction of one...he is offensive to many Native Americans and those of us who are not. And although he can be moving at half-time of a basketball game, the bigger issue is much more important than that and the Illini Nation of fans and Alumni should all be able to see where the problem lies, and let him be retired in peace.
October 1, 2009 at 11:33am

Tim Kirby - *The reason I used the cowboys instead of another mascot was as a play on the child hood game of "Cowboys and Indians" implying cowboys were responsible for the Native American suffering. Again, that was to be intentionally absurd.*
October 1, 2009 at 11:33am ·

Jason Barham - Phil, he is not offensive to most Native Americans. In fact, he offends more non-Natives than Native-Americans as a whole.
October 1, 2009 at 11:34am

Jammin' Jimmy Bean - Jason, I was gonna leave it alone, but you know me. Your last statement speaks VOLUMES. If people are aware and continue to offend anyway, then they are being malicious in my book.
October 1, 2009 at 11:35am

Jason Barham - Jim, that begs the question: should everything that offends SOMEONE be banned? At what point does the majority hold more sway than the vocal minority?
October 1, 2009 at 11:36am

Phil Strang - Well that question always arises. How many people is it okay to offend? Should we set a %? As for what % of Native Americans are offended, I have no way to measure. I could say all the ones I know and that would be accurate. My gf in Michigan is Native American and her tribe is pretty much in agreement on this issue. As are many people who have spoken on campus in the past ten years. But of course there are always opposing opinions in every

group.
October 1, 2009 at 11:46am

Tim Kirby - *Phil, as a non-Native American you have the right to disapprove of the chief. However for non-Native Americans to say they are "offended" is a little over the top. Unless you are part of the group you cannot claim to understand the mindset. There are many things much more ingrained in society that are much more offensive to most of us. I will bet your grade school teacher taught you the word squaw for woman. The actual translation is closer to the "c" word. How do you feel about the FL Seminoles? Their mascot is not a real Native American but they have the blessing of the Seminole nation. By your logic they too should change.*
October 1, 2009 at 11:53am

Tim Kirby - *"tribe"??*
October 1, 2009 at 11:55am

Tim Kirby - *Damn Jim, look what you started. I am gonna bow out now because none of us will ever change anyone else's mind. Thanks Jim, Jason, John and Phil for a spirited debate and exercise in free speech.*
October 1, 2009 at 12:01pm

Phil Strang - Tim...perhaps I am a little too easily offended... a white boy dressed up as a Chief offends me, a white man dressed in black face offends me, the President of Iran saying the Holocaust was made up offends me. The war in Vietnam offended me. But I am not offended by other people's opinions. As a matter of fact I love a good debate.

My girlfriend lives on a reservation in Northern Michigan, do you find the term tribe offensive?
October 1, 2009 at 12:06pm

Phil Strang - That Jim Bean sure is a trouble maker and a rabble rouser. No offense meant to anyone.
October 1, 2009 at 12:09pm

Jammin' Jimmy Bean - It's Florida State that uses the Seminole mascot. They have permission from the tribe and they compensate the tribe for it. Two things the U of I does not and cannot do because there is no longer an Illiniwek tribe. Good debate gentlemen. I will resume focusing on raising MY level of awareness. Namaste.
October 1, 2009 at 12:16pm

Jammin' Jimmy Bean - Just a side note Tim, I'm not black, but listening to my father use racial slurs offends the f**k out of me. So much so that I spend very little time with him.
October 1, 2009 at 12:21pm

Jammin' Jimmy Bean - Thanks Phil, that's the nicest thing anyone has said about me today.
October 1, 2009 at 12:37pm

Chris Goodrow - Wow. Now this is an interesting conversation. It looks like Jim's original post was not asking whether you are for or against the Chief as a mascot, but rather if you are for it, does it also mean you are in favor of bringing back the third Reich and slavery. If it wasn't so absurd, I'd be offended by the jump from one thing to the other.

131

While the atrocities done to the Native Americans (and many other people throughout the world since then) by this country were horrendous, I hardly think that people who are "pro chief" condone what I like to refer to as genocide to the Native Americans. Does having the chief as a mascot take away from those atrocities? Does it make any of it ok? I certainly think not. Like Tim said, the Chief is not a reflection of that. Isn't the debate more of the fact that it isn't really an accurate depiction of an Illini chief? The use of the chief as a mascot to me doesn't dismiss the suffering of the Native Americans. I'd say it's more the growing apathy and lack of truth in this country that is more at fault than a football mascot.

Now, to the point of what is offensive? You know who knows best on what is offensive? The person who is offended. Where do we draw the line between genuinely offended and overly sensitive? I mean, come on, Jim, there are hundreds or even thousands of songs that people would or could consider offensive. Would you still sing them? If you did, would that make you malicious? Or is it only malicious if you agree and understand the offense? See, I honestly don't think people who are "pro chief" see it as offensive. I honestly don't know which is right or wrong. Being a public school, probably better to err on the side of caution, however.

And Tim, while I can somewhat agree that not being part of a group makes it difficult to understand the mindset, I can't get behind the idea that I'm over the top in being offended at harms being done to groups I'm not a part of.
October 1, 2009 at 12:47pm

132

Tim Kirby - *I do not find tribe upsetting. I was just pointing out how one thing can be offensive and another innocuous. The first Americans did not use the word tribe. That was the whites. Jim of course everyone can be offended by anything they choose. Perhaps I went a little too far with that as got into the debate. I assure everyone I meant no "offense". :-) Again, thanks to all. You have made my day fly by. I think I will agree to disagree. Jim, Namaste*

October 1, 2009 at 12:51pm ·

Scott Murphy - Those of you involved in this debate may find this link of interest.

<link removed>

October 1, 2009 at 1:12pm

Jammin' Jimmy Bean - Chris, that's an interesting interpretation of my original post but not true. How hypocritical of me would it be to offend people while trying to enlighten them about offending others? I used The Third Reich and slavery as issues of atrocity that hopefully we can all agree were solved. Once solved, not many people want to have what used to be, I hope. The Chief issue had been solved and instead of letting the wounds heal over time, the pro-Chief folks can't seem to let go.

I do edit and modify my set when I play acoustically so as not to harm or offend and I refuse to do songs romanticizing drug or alcohol abuse in our band.

As for those who do not see racial stereotypes as harmful and offensive I offer this Buddhist proverb and philosophy.........."Ignorance is the cause of all suffering."

133

This has been a wonderfully civil debate and I bow to you all for joining or just reading. Namaste.
October 1, 2009 at 1:28pm

Jammin' Jimmy Bean - Thanks Scott, very informative.
October 1, 2009 at 1:46pm

Tim Kirby - *I thought I was done but now I have to comment on Jim's comment. It was the civility of this that made it enjoyable. It is nice to have a discussion on such a volatile issue and not be called names by the other side and not have people who agree with me start name calling and make me look like a dunderhead by association. Perhaps if more people behaved this way more could be accomplished. Kudos to everyone and big thanks to Jim for starting us out. The Buddha also said "All life is suffering"*
October 1, 2009 at 1:47pm

November 11, 2006 – Veteran's Day and Islam

Jammin' Jimmy Bean - I am a veteran of the U.S. Navy but please don't thank me today. I am opposed to the wars we are involved in and my thoughts today are about all the lives lost. Fighting for peace is like fucking for birth control!
November 11, 2009 at 11:52am

Nicole Wood - U amaze me sometimes
November 11, 2009 at 11:57am

WileyDeb Weddle - I support those in harm's way and who really do believe or have they are fighting for something but

as to today's wars, I am very much opposed to. Lots of young kids with no money, few options are getting killed and maimed in the name of greed.
November 11, 2009 at 12:01pm

Bob Zimmerman - Well the problem is other people want to kill us. The 9/11 commission said radical Islam was at war with us. We were not at war with them. Last week a radical Muslim gunned down 13 people at Ft. Hood. They are at war with us and with have to fight back. Like it or not. I thank all vets today for their service to the country. You to Jim
November 11, 2009 at 12:02pm

Zack Widup - A brilliant man from the Netherlands has been trying to tell the USA for over 20 years that a war with radical Islam cannot be fought as a military battle. It has to be fought as a propaganda war. Unless we start sending suicide bombers of our own into their camps. I don't like that idea.
November 11, 2009 at 12:10pm

Bob Zimmerman - We don't need to do that Zack but we need to stop all the political correct nonsense.
November 11, 2009 at 12:14pm

Jammin' Jimmy Bean - Thanks for making my point Bob. All the troops, bombs, ships, and planes we've sent overseas couldn't stop one lunatic on our own land. Maybe it's time to address the real problem and perhaps find a real solution. Enemies don't grow on trees, they happen due to circumstances and miscommunication. Have you ever been

pissed at someone for no reason? If you feel wronged it is because of an action, not a belief. It's called cause and effect. Are you paranoid? I don't feel any danger from Islam, maybe I'm just too ignorant to understand that people are out to get me. I find the biggest threat today to be corruption and lies from the very people that are supposed to keep us protected. I don't really need any help in the protection area. I am prepared to die and therefore I don't live in fear of it.
November 11, 2009 at 12:21pm

Bill Gorrell - Right on Jim! Our problems with Islamic people are the legacy of European colonialism and our current imperialism. Instead of creating an Apollo-type program to create a carbon-free nation after the 1973 oil embargo, we elected (I didn't vote for the ass) the affable dunce Ronald Reagan in 1980 so he could take the solar panels off of the White House under orders from the oil industry.
November 11, 2009 at 12:38pm

Bob Zimmerman - Jim you don't understand the radical Islamic terrorism. We could bring all the troops home and they would still be at war with us. The goal for them is worldwide Sharia Law. We they come here and gun down pregnant woman and fly planes into buildings you better have some fear of them.
November 11, 2009 at 12:53pm

Bob Zimmerman - Bill you don't get it either.
November 11, 2009 at 12:55pm

Bob Zimmerman - Jim if you are not worried about yourself worry about your family.
November 11, 2009 at 1:00pm

Bill Gorrell - Saying that I don't get it doesn't refute my argument. I'm sure that there are some Muslims here and elsewhere who hate us and our culture, just as Timothy McVeigh, a Christian America, hated us and our culture. I don't believe that a substantial number or Muslims or Christian Americans want to do us harm. However, there are now many thousands of people in Iraq and Afghanistan who had nothing to do with any terrorism who now have good reason to hate us after we killed their friends and relatives and destroyed their property.
November 11, 2009 at 1:04pm

Bill Gorrell - I'm more worried about what the greed heads in Washington and on Wall Street are doing.
November 11, 2009 at 1:05pm

Bob Zimmerman - Bill many people in Iraq and Afghanistan are glad we came too. Bill if you are more worried about Wall Street than people in this country who will walk into a room and mow down people or fly planes into buildings, you really don't understand.

You better understand the threat we face.
November 11, 2009 at 1:08pm

Zack Widup - We won the Revolutionary War against Britain partly because we used different tactics than they did. They marched out in lines in bright red uniforms with drums blazing and we hid behind trees and rocks and shot at them. They were unwilling to "stoop so low" as to use our tactics.

In the same way, we would lose a military battle against extremist Islam because they are willing to use covert and deadly tactics we don't want to "stoop so low" as to use ourselves. They are fighting a completely different type of war than we are. Some people seem to have a hard time admitting that for some reason.
November 11, 2009 at 1:10pm

Bill Gorrell - The actions of the greed heads cause others to hate us through their exploitation of foreign resources, their support of tyrants who abuse their people in service to the greed heads, and their lack of respect for others' cultures.
November 11, 2009 at 1:13pm

WileyDeb Weddle - Bob, I read, respect and try to educate myself about your views. I can't say I agree with bringing / mentioning a man's family / daughters to emphasize your point or to incite fear. Isn't that part of the whole problem?
November 11, 2009 at 1:14pm

Bill Gorrell - I have no family. Never married or had children. I guess that means I'm not worth worrying about.
November 11, 2009 at 1:16pm

James C. Dobbs - Frankly, gentlefolk, I am afraid the truth is worse than what you are thinking on either side of this argument. I think that the Radical Islamists are a clear and present danger to every American, AND that we are taking it in the ass from the very elected officials who are supposed to be acting in our best interests. I support the troops, but detest the war and the policies that have locked us into it. As far as Muslims amongst us - they are indeed a "Fifth Column" that is perfectly positioned to wreak terrorist havoc right here at home. I am embarrassed that we set up internment camps for Japanese-Americans during WWII, because it goes against the very freedoms we are out to protect and which we cherish. The Muslim thing is even harder because people of all races are Muslim, and as I said it would be wrong to move against any "group" or "classification" of people because it would violate the fundamental tenets of our free society.

As you can see, I agree with alarmists on both sides, but I have no solutions in mind, either.

Be excellent to each other.

November 11, 2009 at 1:19pm

Bob Zimmerman - Debbie people should be worried about this. The Ft. Hood shooter was in contacted with al Qaeda. He was In the same Mosque as the 9/11 hijackers. The FBI and others looked the other way because they were afraid to offend Muslim. Debbie this is not a game.

Ok I will use my family. I worry about my kids. My wife. My family.

November 11, 2009 at 1:19pm

Jammin' Jimmy Bean - I have been able to protect my family quite well against the boogie man for many years now. I don't live in fear and as a matter of fact I fear nothing. After my mom was murdered I realized that NOTHING could happen to me in this life any worse than

139

that. I made it through that time in my life and I plan to outlive any enemies I have made in this life. I made a vow on my mother's grave to protect my daughters from being abused, so far I've been very lucky and successful at that, and will continue to until my last breath.
November 11, 2009 at 1:19pm

Bob Zimmerman - The only problem is we are not dealing with the "boogie man". That is not who gunned down people at Ft. Hood. It was a radical Muslim. We have to face this problem and deal with it. That is all I'm saying and it does not mean attacking Wall Street or the oil companies.
November 11, 2009 at 1:21pm

Tim Kirby - *The war against radical Islam can be won in one way only that I see. Drop a tactical nuke on Mecca and Medina, and let Israel take back the Temple Mount. That would show that we mean business and that we will stop at nothing to win. That said, obviously we CAN'T do that because it would be the most inhumane act since the holocaust, so we better get used to the idea that there will never be a middle ground. The Muslims hate our way of life, we don't understand theirs. I guess you could say in a way I am advocating the isolationism of the past. However, I am all about Israel defending themselves without interference from our government and if they want to express their sovereignty back taking back the site of Solomon's Temple then I am with them. And before anyone flames me about the land belonging to the "Palestinians", they are all refugees from Jordan and have no historic or legal claim to the land. Let Jordan cede some*

land to them for a state if it is so important to the Arab community.
November 11, 2009 at 1:23pm •

Bob Zimmerman - Well said James. Both republicans and democrats have not dealt with this problem. I wonder how many Americas will have to die before the country wakes up?
November 11, 2009 at 1:23pm

Bill Gorrell - Jim Dobbs, you have the solution, "Be excellent to each other." If you are worried about Muslims in America, quit doing unnecessary things that piss them off. I actually more worry about right-wing Christians in America.

I vow to protect anyone's daughters, and sons for that matter, if I can. I plan to become a bodhisattva so I also vow to help all sentient beings achieve enlightenment before I get off of the wheel of karma.
November 11, 2009 at 1:27pm

Sherrin Fitzer - Yes Bill!
November 11, 2009 at 1:32pm

Bill Gorrell - Tim, there is no "the Muslims" but there are millions of Muslim individuals with varying points of view, including many here in the United States who love our culture and are patriots. I am all for Israel defending itself and I don't see how the U.S. is interfering with it. We actually give them $10 billion a year as a bribe to keep them from attacking Arab nations. I am against Israel treating the Palestinians like we treated the First Americans. Even Goldstone, a Jewish judge who has described himself as a

Zionist, has condemned Israel's actions.
November 11, 2009 at 1:33pm

Bob Zimmerman -Bill again you don't get it. If right wing Christians are more of a threat to you than radical Muslims you are just plan nuts. The OK city bomber was a not a right wing Christian. There is a Middle East connection there too but the government has covered it up.

Millions and millions of Christians do not hurt anyone and really do a lot to feed, house and give medical attention to people who need it.

Most Muslims live in the 4th century. They treat goats better than they do women. Wake up
November 11, 2009 at 1:34pm

WileyDeb Weddle - It is the right-wing Christians that I distrust the most. Have a good day!
November 11, 2009 at 1:34pm

Bob Zimmerman - Yes Debbie they are such bad people!! God help this country!!
November 11, 2009 at 1:35pm

Bill Gorrell - I'm done on this thread. Have a good day, all of you.
November 11, 2009 at 1:41pm

Jason Barham - Supporting the troops and thanking a Veteran has nothing to do with whether you agree with military conflicts that we're engaged in.
November 11, 2009 at 1:41pm

WileyDeb Weddle - Bob, My family and I have been attacked by some radical right wing so called Christians. We lost everything we cared about and I am not talking about money and material things. They are located in Urbana, Il.. I still believe in God and goodness so there really must be miracles. Bye all :)
November 11, 2009 at 1:50pm

Tim Kirby - *OK Bill, I assume you mean those great Muslim-American patriots like Maj. Nidal Malik Hasan, Louis Farrakhan and the great draft dodger "Muhammad Ali (who, for the record I am a big fan of his skill, just not his politics)?*

The Obama administration has threatened Israel if they attack Iran, whose President has said over and over that Israel needs to be "wiped from the map". Apparently we have a different idea of what Israel protecting themselves means. If you really want to know what is going on over there, try turning off the Obama propaganda channel CNN and picking up a copy of the Jerusalem Post.

There is no comparison of the treatment of "Palestinians" and of "First Americans". By definition the First Americans were here first. As I said previously, the Palestinians were sent into Israel from their native Jordan after the establishment of the Jewish state. There is NO historic nation of Palestine, never was. I think a better comparison would be the treatment of Jews by their Arab neighbors.

143

I need an entire post concerning Goldstone. It will follow shortly.
November 11, 2009 at 1:53pm

Jimmy Lariviere - The problem, friends, is that our elected officials have entrenched us in a thousand year old war over religious beliefs that we have no business being in. The sentiment of the day is the remembrance of those who, when told by their government to defend the principles of their country, didn't ask why they simply put their lives on the line regardless of their political views. Jim, I think if you don't want the thanks, you have earned the right to ignore them simply because at the time you would have given your life if it had been necessary. Whether you agree with wars or not, our troops deserve your support.
November 11, 2009 at 1:53pm

Bob Zimmerman - and that is the point Debbie "so called Christians" I have no idea what you mean by attack. But feel free to send me a PM. i have to leave now. Have a good day
November 11, 2009 at 1:54pm

Jammin' Jimmy Bean - I love it when you ask someone how they support the troops. (Usually a dead silence follows) Support takes more than a bumper sticker and applauding when someone says support the troops. I support the troops by demanding that we quit sending young kids to die so that a few old farts can make a bunch of money!
November 11, 2009 at 1:59pm

Chris Goodrow - It's quite obvious that the propaganda machine that the United States government keeps well-oiled is doing its job rather well. During the Soviet-Afghan war, the United States financed and armed the Mujahedeen which eventually pushed the Russians out of Afghanistan. The Mujahedeen was made up of Muslims including Osama Bin Laden (notice how we had a hand in bringing this monster around). We also had a hand in helping bring the Taliban into power. (Our good ideas never cease, do they?)

For some reason we never had much of a problem with the Muslims at that time, because the propaganda at that time had a meaner and bigger enemy known as Russia. At that time, any enemy of Russia was a friend of ours. It wasn't just in Afghanistan where Reagan played the puppeteer.

Does anyone remember why we initially went into Afghanistan? We demanded that the Taliban hand over Osama Bin laden. They actually wanted some sort of evidence. At the time, we were working the "we know he's guilty" argument and "we'll come and get him if you don't give him to us". Only the United States can get away with that bold of a move. We also wanted the Taliban out of power (remember who helped them get there?). We still don't have Osama and the Taliban continues to move around (they do that, they don't live in mansions). Can someone explain what our end game is in Afghanistan at this point?
November 11, 2009 at 2:00pm

Jammin' Jimmy Bean - Oh yeah! In my opinion right wing Christians are the most hypocritical and uninformed people walking the planet.
November 11, 2009 at 2:03pm

Jammin' Jimmy Bean - My mom was a Christian who believed God would keep her safe. Where was God the night her throat was slit from ear to ear in her sleep? You can believe whatever you want but I think relying on imaginary friends to watch over you is a bit naive.
November 11, 2009 at 2:16pm

Jammin' Jimmy Bean - This is borrowed...........As Andy Andrist stated at a show one time: What do most of these people do for them? And putting a bumper sticker on yr. car and clapping at my "Support the troops" statement doesn't count. The dead silence that ensued was classic.
November 11, 2009 at 2:20pm

Bill Gorrell - I've noticed that we're arguing with different sets of "facts." I don't watch CNN or MSNBC or any other news channels. My news comes from sources much farther left than the MSM. For example, I listen to "Democracy Now" which a few years ago had our host, JJB, on to tell about his problems with Carle.

Anyway, we're not going to solve this, only the Israelis and Palestinians can do that. I hope they do for their own sakes if for no other reason. Every human being deserves a safe and secure life unless they harm others.
November 11, 2009 at 2:26pm

Amy Irle - I wasn't silent! Couldn't you hear me from there?
November 11, 2009 at 2:31pm

Tim Kirby - *Onto the Goldstone Report. Goldstone is from South Africa not from Israel, and has had his sights on the Sec. Gen. of the UN. So much so that his colleagues on the*

146

bench in S.A. call him Richard Richard Goldstone in reference to Boutros Buotros Ghali. And his report was done for the UN which has a decidedly anti-Israeli if nor out right anti-Semitic leaning. And the report has been proven to be composed of outright lies and half-truths.

-ISRAEL DELIBERATELY TARGETED PALESTINIAN CIVILIANS. False. The IDF dropped thousands of warning leaflets, made over 200,000 telephone warnings to Palestinian civilians, aborted missile strikes to prevent civilian casualties, and opened a field clinic for Palestinians on the Gaza border.

-THE REPORT FOUND NO EVIDENCE OF PALESTINIANS USING HUMAN SHIELDS. False. Even the Palestinians admit to it. "For the Palestinian people death became an industry at which women excel and so do all people on this land. The elderly excel, the Jihad fighters excel, and the children excel. Accordingly Palestinians created a human shield of women, children, the elderly and Jihad fighters against the Zionist bombing machine, as if they were saying to the Zionist enemy, we desire death as you desire life." - Fahti Hamad, Member, Palestinian Legislative Council, Hamas Al-Aqsa TV, Feb 29 2008

-THE GOLDSTONE REPORT IS OBJECTIVE AND UNTAINTED BY BIAS OR POLITICIZATION. False. It was clear that one out of the four members of the Goldstone Mission, Professor Christine Chinkin, had already made up her mind, having signed a letter before the conflict had even ended, clearly stating that Israel's actions in Gaza amounted to "war crimes" and that Palestinian rocket attacks were not

147

significant enough for Israel to exercise her right to self-defense.

-THERE IS NO REASON TO DOUBT THE RELIABILITY OF "EYEWITNESSES" AND NGOs. False. The case of Khaled and Kawthar Abed Rabbo, as outlined by CAMERA, offers ample evidence of unreliable witnesses. While the Goldstone committee "found Khalid and Kawthar Abd Rabbo to be credible and reliable witnesses [and] has no reason to doubt the veracity of the main elements of their testimony," Khaled Abd Rabbo and his relatives have given more than a dozen different versions of what happened to them on Jan. 7, 2009.

In addition, as evidenced in the above case, Goldstone failed to take into account the loyalties of different Palestinian factions and the incentive for Fatah or Hamas members to blame Israeli soldiers for killings that were actually part of intra-Palestinian violence.

Let's finish with the words of Britain's Colonel Richard Kemp, a former commander of the British forces in Afghanistan. In a statement to the UN Human Rights Council, he declared that, 'based on my knowledge and experience, I can say this: During Operation Cast Lead, the Israeli Defense Forces did more to safeguard the rights of civilians in a combat zone than any other army in the history of warfare. More than anything, the civilian casualties were a consequence of Hamas' way of fighting. Hamas deliberately tried to sacrifice their own civilians. Israel had no choice apart from defending its people, to stop Hamas from attacking them with rockets'. The Goldstone Commission could have seized the opportunity to examine the phenomenon of asymmetrical warfare and make a serious contribution to an issue that will provide a huge challenge for the West in the coming decades.

Warren Goldstein, the chief rabbi of South Africa who, incidentally, has a PhD in human rights law, described the mission as a 'sham' which demonstrated a 'complete lack of integrity and fairness... It looks like law,' he declared, 'but it is not. It is just politics'. Closer to home, a longstanding family friend of Goldstone wrote to him in blunt language: the report, she said, 'did not arise from ignorance or naivety. I am trying so hard to resist the conclusion that your role and report might represent a self-serving desire to ingratiate yourself for a more senior position in the... United Nations. If true – and one hopes that this is not the case – at what price'?

Basically, Goldstone cut himself off from his Zionist roots when it was convenient for his political future just like he did when he separated himself from apartheid just before it fell so as to position himself better in the new regime.

So there is your "self-professed" Zionist.
November 11, 2009 at 2:48pm

Jimmy Lariviere - You're right Jim. It IS about more than bumper stickers. It's about not repeating the treatment of the Vietnam vets. It's about getting those kids home and readjusted to a "normal" life so they aren't sitting in a tower waiting for a clear shot....
November 11, 2009 at 2:48pm

Tim Kirby - *Jim, we need to have a talk sometime about Gnosticism and Gnostic Christianity. We can have such a talk now without being burned as heretics. It is more of a dualist religion. It puts Satan on pretty much an even footing with Yahweh. It prescribes that creation is flawed because it was made by a lesser creator god. Not by an all-powerful supreme god, basically the Gods of the old and new testament. It goes a long way towards explaining the evil you have faced and the disease that I have face. That has always been my question, how can a benevolent god allow such things to go on in the world and why do good people suffer while the wicked do not. I was not ready to completely abandon my Christian roots because I see so many things in the world that cannot in my mind be accidents on a cosmic scale. The hard to be some intelligent design. But like I said there were enough bad things also that I could not wrap my head around a "perfect" creation. After I discovered the Cathars from the middle ages and their teachings everything kind of came into focus. I realize it is kind of strange to study and practice a "dead" religious sect from 1000 years ago, but who knows they may have survived and become dominant had it not been for the hegemony of "THE" church and their inquisition. I guess the best way I could describe Gnosticism to you, Jim, is try to imagine Jesus Christ and Siddhartha Gautama sitting down over coffee and trying to come up with the "theory of everything".*
November 11, 2009 at 3:03pm

Amy Irle - I would much prefer a conversation about Gnocchi, but that's just me.
November 11, 2009 at 3:04pm

Tim Kirby - *Fair enough Bill. Since you admit that perhaps your news comes from the left I will admit that mine comes from the right. I think perhaps we are both smart enough however to realize that neither of us could possibly be entirely wrong and neither could be entirely correct, and that the truth is probably somewhere in the middle. And I would have to agree that a few opinionated, vocal folks on a website have no chance of solving a 6000 year old conflict, but wouldn't it be great if we could.*
November 11, 2009 at 3:08pm

Tim Kirby - *BTW Jim, you have an unusual group of friends. About the only things that we all have in common is a passion for our beliefs (which fall all over the spectrum from Libertarian to Socialist and from Anarchist to Communist) and our undying love and respect for the great Jammin' Jimmy Bean.*
November 11, 2009 at 3:12pm

Amy Irle - Tim, you forgot a coupla groups. I belong to the group that refuses to be sucked into Internet Drama and would rather just have fun with life. Enjoy -- and go make some Gnocchi for cryin' out loud. Now I'm hungry again. Great.
November 11, 2009 at 3:14pm

Tim Kirby - *Amy, I didn't forget your group; you are the folks who are passionate about life. :-)*
November 11, 2009 at 3:24pm

Mark Fredericks - Hey Jim, i just want to thank you for using your powers for good on this planet...
November 11, 2009 at 4:25pm

Tracie Castle-Mcdade - I did not know you are a veteran. Impressed!!!
November 11, 2009 at 6:52pm

Tracie Castle-Mcdade - Oh, and i read the previous posts, i agree with you Jim (Jimmy? what do you prefer?) wholeheartedly.... the entire fiasco our world is in boils down to a nice rue of greed and our country is first in line.
November 11, 2009 at 7:00pm

Elizabeth Shafer - I have not read all the 55 posts that everyone has written about, since your original status this morning but one thing i can say as an OPERATION IRAQI FREEDOM VET!! When you say that you support the troops that means you have to support the war that we are fighting because when we are over there doing what we have to do.. seeing the media bs that goes on here and there and as a young soldier we need to know that our country supports the efforts that are being put forth by us.... so please if you do or don't support the war then at that moment in time you are deciding to or not to support us the new generation of combat veterans it's that simple...You may want everyone to come home so do i and I wish to God that my friends did not have to die or come

152

home different from when we left but at the same time that is something we choose. WE made that choice because we believe in a greater good and want to see justice for those who deserve it. oooh and Mr. Bean weather you want it or not thank you for your service to this great country which allows us to listen to your great music...be thankful you live here and not there.....
November 11, 2009 at 7:31pm

Bill Gorrell - Tim, I find your post about Gnosticism fascinating. I was interested in it before I settled on Buddhism, where good, bad, and indifferent events are caused by karma which is created by the choices you made when confronted by earlier karma.
November 11, 2009 at 8:23pm

Bill Gorrell - Tim, I'm also fascinated by JJB's group of friends.
November 11, 2009 at 8:25pm

Jimmy Lariviere - I'll give you credit - when you stir the pot, you still do it with the same vigor you always did......
lmao......
November 11, 2009 at 9:53pm

Bill Gorrell - Cause and effect.
November 11, 2009 at 10:31pm

Jammin' Jimmy Bean - Elizabeth's comment really took me back. I've known her since she was a child and remember when I was told she was going overseas that my heart sank. I'm so glad she is safe today and hope she understands that

153

I do support the troops but not the cause. You'd be hard-pressed to find someone more willing to fight, for the right cause, than me.
November 11, 2009 at 10:41pm

Jammin' Jimmy Bean - Spoken like a true scholar! (^:
November 11, 2009 at 11:08pm

Jammin' Jimmy Bean - Jeff, if you have a point to make I'd love to hear it. You jumped in calling my thread a Pot of Bullshit, with nothing to back it up. I have a suggestion: if the truth hurts too much quit reading my posts. What branch of the service were you in?
November 12, 2009 at 7:00am

March 11, 2009 – Rush Limbaugh

Jammin' Jimmy Bean - Rush Limbaugh says if the health care insurance reforms are enacted he'll move to Costa Rica. REALLY? That's the smartest plan he's ever had, and the only thing he's ever said that I would agree with. One less hypocrite is a good start! He will only be missed by fools.
March 11 at 7:18pm

WileyDeb Weddle - Costa Rica? Wonder why .... That is not a poor place ....
March 11 at 7:20pm

Christine Epley-Sorenson - :)~~~~~~~~~~~~~~~~~ I wouldn't mind just visiting somewhere nice and warm right now. I

don't care about Rush. Just let me win the lotto and make a village/ commune and I am good (kool-aide is not aloud)
March 11 at 7:29pm

Jammin' Jimmy Bean -This from the man who claims to be loyal and patriotic. This country would be better off without him in my opinion. I certainly don't listen to him but can't help but hear his latest tirades as reported weekly in the news.
March 11 at 7:46pm

Ethan Deppe - I want those insurance reforms, but if for some crazy reason I didn't, I'd vote them through just to get Rush Limbaugh the hell away from us.
March 11 at 7:46pm

Andy Crownover - Anything we can do to get him to leave the country, I am ALL for.........
March 11 at 7:56pm

WileyDeb Weddle - I looked up what I thought. Costa Rica has one of the oldest socialized medical programs ever. Many Americans go there for medical care. What an asshole Rush is!
March 11 at 7:59pm

Steve Friedrich - You have it wrong. He said he would go to Costa Rica for health care, not to move there. I think the country would be much better off if Obama decided to leave.
March 11 at 8:01pm

Steve Friedrich - And take Ried ,Pelosi ,Durbin and Andy Stern, too.
March 11 at 8:12pm

Chris Green - Remember when Rush got caught going to Costa Rica before with someone else's Viagra prescription??? Maybe he's just horny again. Either that or he just wants to skip out on paying US taxes and broadcast from down there.
March 11 at 8:31pm

Eddie Rawdin - I wish the a..wipe would move farther than that.
March 11 at 8:40pm

Michael Enoch - Glen Beck, Rush Limbaugh and Sean Hannity should just shut the f*** up!
March 11 at 9:11pm

Jammin' Jimmy Bean - @ Steve, I was only conveying the message that is to the right of the page on Facebook. I have no way of knowing what Rush says because I NEVER listen to him. My time is more valuable to me than that.
March 11 at 9:17pm

Tim Kirby -*@Jim, I get that you disagree with the Right and that is totally cool, everyone should have their own opinion and that should not be taken away. However, "I certainly don't listen to him but can't help but hear his latest tirades as reported weekly in the news" is not good. Rush is often misquoted in the media so mostly you are* getting a false impression of what was said, not that you would agree with the accurate quote either. :-)

"He will only be missed by FOOLS." This comment is beneath you. One of the things I have admired about you is that you are able to debate an issue without resorting to name calling. You are too good for that. I have always taken you as someone who respects the person even if you don't respect the position they hold.

"This country would be better off without him in my opinion" this is more like it. You are stating an opinion without denigrating others for theirs (besides Rush I mean).

@Michael "Glen Beck, Rush Limbaugh and Sean Hannity should just shut the f*** up" I am glad to see that you are such a firm supporter of the first amendment. I understand that you disagree with the people you mentioned, but they have a right to speak, just the same as you do here. The do NOT however have the right to be heard. If you don't like what they say, follows Jim's advice, don't listen.

@Steve, while I agree with you that Obama, Pelosi, Reid, et al are most certainly a problem, I don't think running people out of the country is the answer, just out of office. Besides, our side is supposed to be the more grown up, the one that sticks to the issues and doesn't resort to silliness.

One last thing, I am not EVEN going to touch the health care thing on here. I am going to get flamed bad enough over this.

To all of you thank you for allowing me MY freedom of speech. And for the few of you who actually made it all the way through this dreck, thanks for allowing me to be heard.

Sorry, one more last thing then I will get off my soap box. Just remember, Conservative, Liberal, Democrat, Republican, Libertarian, Socialist, Communist, Fascist, Tea Bagger, or Nazi, We are ALL American.

March 11 at 11:57pm

Tim Kirby - *I am headed over to Twitter where I can just be funny*

March 11 at 11:59pm

Jammin' Jimmy Bean - "A conservative is a man who believes that nothing should be done for the first time." - Alfred E. Wiggam

March 12 at 12:38am

Tim Kirby - *A quote about conservatism from the turn of the last century doesn't have a lot of relevance today. The meaning has changed drastically over the last hundred years. Besides wisdom from a man who only has the one quote cited to him on the entire web???*

March 12 at 12:48am

Tim Kirby - *Not to mention, kind of off topic since the rest of the thread was more about free speech. Although I guess it is your thread so you can change it up.*

March 12 at 12:50am

Joshua Hartke - @Tim -- "while I agree with you that Obama, Pelosi, Reid, et al are most certainly a problem, I don't think running people out of the country is the answer, just out of office"

So you disagree with the rights of the people to elect whom they wish to office? Or do you disagree with Obama et. al.'s right to free speech?

And you can try to pull the "misquoted" card on Rush, but that dog won't hunt. Even the smallest listen to Rush's show proves his misogyny, racism, and fear-mongering, as well as his ignorance of economics, diplomacy, and the reality of people who don't have $300 million contracts.

Do you think Rush is aware of the fact that Costa Rica has a nationalized health care system?
March 12 at 10:47am

Tim Donaldson - I would like to start a new Facebook page that prohibits any political talk on Facebook. The old saying is so true. "Don't discuss money, religion, or politics with friends, if you want to remain friends.
March 12 at 11:05am

Joshua Hartke - Here's a more current quote that you might find more relevant: "There's class warfare, all right, but it's my class, the rich class, that's making war, and we're winning." -- Warren Buffet, 2006
March 12 at 11:31am

Tim Kirby -@*Joshua thank you for proving my point that the left cannot help but misquote. At no point did I say I disagree with people's right to elect who they wish. I think only someone who was trying to distort what I said would*

159

read anything into the statement other than I was saying they needed to be VOTED out of office. If you would care to actually read my post you will notice that I was chiding a fellow conservative at that point for what I saw as silliness. I am also not sure how you came up with my disagreeing with the Dem leadership not having free speech. I believe I said that everyone is entitled to their opinion.

As far as Rush, a quick listen will NOT tell you what you need to know. Limbaugh tends toward humor, not necessarily good humor, but if you only listen briefly you would not get that he is intentionally being absurd, nor will that come across in a news sound bite. You cannot get the context of what someone is saying by listening to one sentence. FYI I do not listen to Rush regularly, only when there is nothing else on. And I do not listen to Glen Beck or Hannity either. But they do have a right to speak as does Chris Matthews and Olbermann. If you do not like it don't listen. You really gave your true feelings away when you mentioned how much Limbaugh makes. Pure jealousy. It upsets you that someone came from a modest background and made himself successful. The left hates the idea of someone succeeding without a government handout. If people realize they can succeed they will also realize they don't need the government. That is why the left propagates class envy.

In the future if you want to debate me I will be more than glad to do it, but do not misquote me and put words into my mouth. By the way.

An apology to all the other lefties on here. We have had some spirited debates in the past and I hope we can *continue to do so. This rant was directed solely at the one who misquoted me.*

I will finish the same way I did last night. Left or Right we are all Americans. And I am sorry that there are a few on BOTH sides that disagree with me on that.
March 12 at 11:37am

Tim Kirby - *All I have to say to the rich people out there with all their money is GOOD FOR YOU. You worked and made something of yourself. More people should do the same. And to paraphrase Spiro T Agnew, listening to wealthy liberals (read: Warren Buffet) complain about inequity is like listening to a germ complain about disease. Joshua, you have made it perfectly clear that you problem is that you are unhappy that there are people with more than you have. Do something about it; don't wait for it to be given to you.*
March 12 at 11:44am

Tim Donaldson - Couldn't have said it better myself, Tim.
March 12 at 12:14pm

Jammin' Jimmy Bean - Tim most people who are "RICH" did not work for their money. You CANNOT earn that kind of money in a lifetime. Please don't lump me in with any group, I think for myself I don't go with the flow. I am NOT a liberal, I consider myself progressive. I believe the quote stands today as did back then. That's my opinion. From a Buddhist perspective, my aim and goal is equality for every sentient being. On a side note I think Tim D. has a good point as this thread has gotten a little more dividing instead of enlightening which was my goal. (By the way, I am not

161

jealous of ANYONE. My life is full of the kind of riches you cannot calculate on paper. Nothin' but love for you bro.) Namaste.

March 12 at 12:19pm

Jammin' Jimmy Bean ....also I agree with Josh on Rush being racist and such and that is why I believe if you are a follower of his you are a fool. In times of trouble Rush would take all his money and leave all of you followers in a cloud of dust. In my opinion he's a douche bag!

March 12 at 12:30pm

Joshua Hartke - My point of quoting you is that you seem to criticize people for saying, perhaps unartfully, that Rush and his ilk are lying. Freedom of speech goes both ways, but lies need to be called out for what they are. As does racism and class warfare, both things Rush clearly tries to instigate through passive-aggressive "satire". And quite often the reality of his opinion slips through most truthfully in his "humor".

Freedom of speech includes the right to tell a fool or liar that you think he should shut up.

As to jealousy, I have learned that happiness is not in materialism, something that I think frees the mind to truly be happy. I think those that focus solely on their wealth are trying to fill some emptiness within themselves with gold and possession.

What I denigrate is those who are wealthy beyond what any person can truly be worth having no concept for how difficult it is to be a working person trying to struggle

162

through this world. His simple misunderstanding of the point of health care reform points to that unawareness.

Or perhaps it points to a very callous, calculated attempt to foment anger in those who follow him religiously, who might actually benefit from parts of this plan. That way they won't think clearly about the fact that their health insurance company is robbing them blind too.

Plus, as to a "quick listen": you say yourself that you "don't listen to Rush regularly", so at what point has one listened to that gasbag long enough to make judgment on his statements?
March 12 at 12:51pm

Deonaha Conlin - Jimmy, I must disagree on Rush being a 'douchebag'. Even a douchebag has a use...
March 12 at 1:13pm

Tim Kirby - *Jim, my jealousy comment was directed solely at the individual who is bringing up wealth and how much income people have. If you felt I was grouping you in that I apologize. However on that same note I have made clear I am not a "follower" of Rush so please don't refer to me as such. Thanks.*

@Joshua either you are misunderstanding me or I am just not making myself clear (or you just don't want to hear) I am not criticizing ANYONE for having an opinion. If you don't like someone or their opinions you have a complete right to say so. If you believe someone is lying, you also have that right. What. I am criticizing are the people who say things like "they should leave" "they should shut up". I am not criticizing anyone for beliefs. I

163

just think everyone should try to be a little more grownup about the way they express them. I completely disagree with you on issues but will never tell you not to express them, just request that you express them with respect.

I think what everyone needs to remember is that Limbaugh is an entertainment show not a news show. (Before you jump me, yes I realize not everyone is entertained). What I would like to see is someone like Chris Mathews admit that he is an entertainer and stop pretending he has a news program. (It goes both ways). As to how long you have to listen to rush I was not saying you need to be a regular listener just that on any statements you take issue with you need to know the context not just the one line sound bite from MSNBC. That goes for everyone on both sides not just Rush. As far as health care reform, I have been resisting even going there, but before you tell me I don't understand, answer this, have you read the 4000 page bill, I haven't. I have to believe none of us actually know what it entails.

March 12 at 1:21pm

Tim Kirby -*Almost forgot, who are you to decide what a person could "truly be worth" a radio host I do listen to regularly was knocking tin just a few years ago for $12000 per year and now makes millions. I say he pulled himself up and deserves whatever he can get. Same for Rush, he wasn't born wealthy. I don't have a ton of money, that is no fault of anyone but myself.*

March 12 at 1:24pm

Tim Kirby -*I'm tapping out. I think we have all said about all there is to say. One more rebuttal from Josh and Jim should wrap it up. I am afraid if we continue down this road things might get to personal and I don't want to say anything too extreme and hurt someone's feelings. And I don't want mine hurt either. There is nothing any of us can say that will cause a conversion from any of the others. So I for one will "agree to disagree". Much love to you all. Even Josh :-)*
March 12 at 1:33pm

Jammin' Jimmy Bean - Tim I haven't read the entire bill however when I have more time I will post what I do know about it and how it will benefit millions of people, especially those unable to fight the good fight for themselves. (The elderly, the indigent, the poor, the middle class, the physically and mentally challenged and so on.) I must agree it is NOT another WIN / WIN for the status quo but remember, those of us who voted Obama in did so primarily because we wanted change. I'll close with this about Rush.........ANYONE who intentionally misleads, lies to and misdirects people the way that he does are as close to pure evil as I would ever want to be near. If it's unintentional, then in my book he's close to delirious. I don't hide that I enjoy smoking marijuana so to be called a "long-haired, maggot infested, dope smoker" by a hypocritical narcotic addict doesn't hurt my feelings, it gives me an opportunity to exercise discipline, forgiveness, and tolerance considering the source. Even The N.F.L. didn't want to be associated with him and that's a league full of thugs. That speaks VOLUMES about his character. I stand by my

165

assessment.....he's is a DOUCHEBAG of the largest order. (IMHO) (^:
March 12 at 1:55pm

Robin Randolph - cool, Now let's all go get Ice Cream!!
March 12 at 10:16pm

March 19, 2010 – Census and Health Care

(Several of Robin Randolph's posts were deleted before I could copy them for this book. I was able to recover all of them but one from my email in order to maintain continuity in this thread and keep everyone's posts in context. The only comment I was unable to recover was Robin's first post that compared folks on the right to Hitler. In the name of full disclosure, at the time of this writing I do not remember the exact wording of the Hitler post. I would also like to add that Robin and I have no issues with each other)

Jammin' Jimmy Bean - I've truly come a long, long way, but, this Census form with the HUGE LETTERING stating "YOUR RESPONSE IS REQUIRED BY LAW" is begging for a FUCK YOU!
March 19 at 4:23pm

Keith Dillman - I thought you were going to go outside and enjoy the weather?!? (hehe) Guess ya must have stopped by the ole bill-box, Huh? I'm with ya on this one tho'! That's all the fuck I wanna hear is about there is another "some shit" I have to do or I'm in trouble! This comes after the guilt trip that if ya don't fill it out your state might not receive its

share of "Government" funding! Them dickhead think that we don't know that they are the ones that always get the $ back in the end anyway! So I am with ya dude! Let's give 'em a big old FUCK YOU! They don't have jail space for us! LOL How in the hell do they think that they can bring us down when we are already here?!?
March 19 at 4:41pm

Jammin' Jimmy Bean - Yup!!!!! I'm always up for some civil disobedience!
March 19 at 5:07pm

Zack Widup - What are we gonna do when Uncle Samuel comes around
Asking for the young one's name
Looking for the print of his hand
For the files in their numbers game
I don't want his chances for freedom to ever be that slim
Let's not tell 'em about him
- Jefferson Starship, Blows Against The Empire
March 19 at 5:12pm

Aleksandra Grkovic Stamenkovich - It's everyone's responsibility to fill it out. That's how they determine what area gets funding for public works improvements. It's like voting. Don't bitch about the results if you don't care enough or are too lazy to respond.
March 19 at 5:13pm

Jammin' Jimmy Bean - The only thing I'm bitching about is "required by law".
March 19 at 5:18pm

Kendell Welch - The census is important, as it determines how we are represented in our government (among other things.) I encourage you to fill it out.

What will you say if you get a letter from the government saying that "YOU ARE REQUIRED BY LAW TO BUY HEALTH INSURANCE!"?
March 19 at 5:49pm

Jammin' Jimmy Bean - Touché. I'd feel the same way, but for the good of all would gladly concede. (As I will with the census.)
March 19 at 5:56pm

Keith Dillman - Sorry Jim, I started all this! I agree the census is important (or at least that's what all the commercials that our government is putting on TV is telling me) and I'll prolly fill mine out being a good citizen who wants to do my part! I also vote and do jury duty! But do ya think that the umpteen...who knows how many illegals, who work in this country, are gonna fill theirs out? Then see where most of the benefits of these programs go! And then what will you say, if you ever wake up, and realize that you're gonna pay for that too! Do people ever really stop think on their own, for their selves? Sometimes I gotta wonder?
March 19 at 6:16pm

Keith Dillman - It's just the point of "BY LAW" was my point also! I would do it anyway but now I (a citizen in a "free" country) am threatened with recourse, if I don't.
March 19 at 6:23pm

Jammin' Jimmy Bean - I concur Chip.
March 19 at 7:53pm

Tim Kirby - *I was going to stay quiet for a change, but I have to ask. @Robin you honestly read all 3000 pages of the bill? I find that a little hard to believe as that would put you one up on 90%of congress. But if you did you are to be commended.*
March 19 at 10:48pm

Robin Randolph - Have you? I watch listen, etc. just like everyone, but what don't do is buy in to the propaganda which is what it is, this not about the people who need HC. This is about $$ when everybody talks nobody listens and nothing gets done. And all the intellectual mumbo jumbo jive @ the end of the day don't Mean Nothin'! Till they sign it on the dotted line. Good day SIR.
March 19 at 11:05pm

Robin Randolph - I SAID GOOD DAY!!
March 19 at 11:05pm

Tim Kirby - *I never said that I have read the bill. You were telling others to read it to find what it entails, so I RESPECTFULLY asked if you had read it. You openly admit that you have not but profess to be know what is in it. You say you "watch and listen" like everyone else but you "don't buy into the propaganda". I would say you are completely buying to the propaganda from the left. If you have not read it, then you must be getting your info from somewhere?? Your response to my simple question was kind of snide, which I have noticed is the typical tactic of*

169

the left when you guys get tripped up on something, like the fact that you don't know what is in the bill. I also notice you seem to think everyone on the right listens to Glen Beck because you mention him in almost every post. Glen Beck is an idiot and does nothing more than give a negative image to the right. I often wonder if he was planted by the left to make us look bad. What I would like to see is a little more research and a lot less name calling on the issue.

-BTW, I am of Jewish descent and find the Hitler comments offensive on SO many levels
March 19 at 11:45pm

Robin Randolph - Tim, you know what say that's the rap left right you need to stop, enough, you have yours i have mine you don't know me and to say what i doing pal i have a mind, don't go there K? Condescending Patronizing Doesn't work well with me so use your babble on someone else and i know lots of Jewish folks, lighten up! With all due Respect
March 20 at 12:19am

Robin Randolph - and by the pal i listen to the President of the United States of America he be very clear on what's in the Bill GOOD DAY!
March 20 at 12:20am

Tim Kirby - *I was neither condescending nor patronizing. Simply trying to determine if you had followed the advice you were giving others, which you admit you were not. If anyone is being condescending it would be you with your trite "Good Day". And it has been my experience that whenever someone says "with all due respect" there is*

170

never any respect in the statement. I, however, was respectful in my original question about reading the bill. I would expect the same courtesy. I never said you did not "have a mind". You were the one saying that anyone who disagreed with your position was "buying to the propaganda". I was merely pointing out that propaganda is a two way street. As far as listening to the President to know what is in the bill, he has dodged the specifics for 12 months so I don't know what you got from him. Besides, I think it is an established fact that Presidents (all politicians) lie. As far as nothing changing if you have insurance, that is patently false. Trust me everyone's taxes WILL go up and that is a pretty big change.

Lastly, I have avoided going personal up to now, but since you opened the door, it seems to me that "I know lots of Jewish folks" is the anti-Semitic equivalent to "I have lots of black friends".

I am done with this thread. You can have the last word if you so wish, but I am moving on. I have said all I have to say on the matter.
March 20 at 12:39am

Robin Randolph - Tim if I have offended you I Apologize it was not my intent, so i wish you well, I am starting immediately a new rule for myself, No Politics on FB It's not worth it when folks start getting their feelings hurt i Would not want it to get out of hand, that's not what FB is in my opinion supposed to be about so Take Care.
March 20 at 12:51am

Jammin' Jimmy Bean - We're all pretty! (^:
March 20 at 1:00am

Tim Kirby - *I guess I'm not done. Thanks for the apology Robin. The only thing offensive was the Hitler thing. The rest of it I thought was just two guys debating an issue that they will never agree on. An exercise in futility, but sporting none the less. So if I went too far I also apologize. Let us agree to disagree and let there be no hard feelings. This time, I am really done with the thread and will not comment on any further posts. And Jim, I love ya man, but these discussions you manage to start are making my hair fall out. Peace out from the far right.*
March 20 at 1:01am

Tim Kirby - *Sorry, last one for real this time. Robin, don't stop debating politics on FB. Everyone should always feel free to express their opinion, even if not everyone agrees. If we don't have debate (fancy word for arguing, right) then we wind up getting complacent. So keep on being a soldier for the left as I will for the right, and perhaps someday we will all meet in the middle. I'm out for real this time.*
March 20 at 1:06am

Jammin' Jimmy Bean - Nice closing Tim, hats off to you sir. Robin is a dear old friend of mine and he and I are quite similar in a LOT of ways. He'll be soldiering one way or another you can be certain of that. I think our debates here are extremely civilized compared to some I have been in. I LOVE your comment........"and perhaps someday will all meet in the middle", The Dalai Lama would love it too. It is

my hope and belief that we ALL shall someday. (^:
March 20 at 1:25am

Robin Randolph – LOVE, LOVE, LOVE, ALL YOU NEED IS
LOVE! Sorry lost my head, Tim you don't me but maybe
someday you will, when i say with all due respect i mean it!
For Real! I do have a bit of a dry sense of humor true but
you can confirm with anyone who knows me for real, I am a
very funny person, and i know you're asking yourself funny
how, funny like the way i talk, or funny like a clown like I'm
here to amuse you, funny how, how am i funny, tell me
what's funny!,, well anyway I have a hell of a sense of
humor to say the least that how i get thru this crazy life
without killing someone,,

   "Again with the Humor" and the Good day was a
reference to that 70's show, and with that i say Good Night
folks tip your waiters and Waitresses were here all week!!
March 20 at 1:41am

Jammin' Jimmy Bean - I think we should debate on who's
funnier, because I am one funny dude...........but looks aren't
everything. (^:
March 20 at 2:12am

Robin Randolph - AMEN BROTHER! And I know funny!
March 20 at 2:18am

March 23, 2010 – Keith Olbermann vs. Conservatives

Jammin' Jimmy Bean - via The Godless Liberal Social Society: Mr. Olbermann nails this like a professional carpenter.

Keith Olbermann Special Comment: GOP Self-Destruction Imminent - 03/22/10
March 23 at 8:37pm

Jammin' Jimmy Bean - If you haven't seen this you really need to, regardless of which side you're on.
March 23 at 9:03pm

Tim Kirby - *Dude, you bash people for listening to Beck and Limbaugh, but you treat Olbermann as gospel. C'mon Jim.*
March 23 at 9:03pm

Tim Kirby - *Before everybody piles on, I am not a big Limbaugh fan and I never listen to Beck. (Glen Beck. I listen to Jeff Beck regularly)*
March 23 at 9:04pm

Scott Murphy - Olbermann is several notches above them in the journalistic integrity game.
March 23 at 9:06pm

Rick Sims - No liberal I know treats Olbermann's rants as gospel. Hell, he's even gone off on Obama. I do agree with him a lot-he's a liberal. I never agree with Beck because he's a self-proclaimed Libertarian (i.e. kookoo conspiracy

theorist) and what liberal could ever agree with Limbaugh?
March 23 at 9:14pm

Tim Kirby - *Scott, Limbaugh is an entertainer/commentator, I think you would agree even if you personally are not entertained. Glen Beck is a little out there; I think we can all agree. But where I have to leave you is Olbermann being a journalist. He is a commentator, not a journalist. As Rick said, Olbermann is a self-professed liberal, and that is fine if that is what you like, but a journalist needs to check his politics at the door and give an unbiased telling of facts. Any "facts" given by either Olbermann or Limbaugh are tainted by their belief system. I think I stated this without being divisive, at least I hope I did because that was my aim. Besides, no matter what side you are on "journalistic integrity" is an oxymoron. :-)*
March 23 at 9:32pm

Tim Kirby - *By the way, I would like to add Rachel Madow in the commentator/non-journalist category. And add Chris "I get a shiver up my leg" Mathews in the Glen Beck out there category.*
March 23 at 9:33pm

Jammin' Jimmy Bean - I post ONE Olbermann clip and I treat him as gospel? I'm not sure what your definition is Tim but it's not the same as most folks I know. I don't believe I bash, if I did wouldn't there be blood?
March 23 at 9:34pm

Tim Kirby - *Sorry Jim, I overstated. You happened to catch me while I was on a roll on someone else's page. But I*

175

think you know what I meant. :-) I have been trying to go a lot more with humor on the political front the 24 hours so I if the "gospel" comment did not come across in the manner intended you have my apology.
March 23 at 9:37pm

Jammin' Jimmy Bean - I'm a progressive by the way. (I hate labels.)
March 23 at 9:39pm

Jammin' Jimmy Bean - @ Tim, did you watch this?
March 23 at 9:43pm

Robin Randolph - Limbaugh an Entertainer?? WTH TIM I don't even know how much of a commentator he is. Radio Personality I'll give that one even though he don't have much personality, He is on the Radio, so I guess he gets a pass, I would like to raise a practical Question??
     Does anybody Remember Laughter!!!
March 23 at 9:44pm

Tim Kirby - *I didn't label you. Never called you a liberal or anything else. Just labeled the media folks that we were discussing.*
March 23 at 9:44pm

Tim Kirby - *Hey Robin, let's not start this again. LOL. I did add a post-script to entertainer that perhaps not everyone was entertained. LOL*
March 23 at 9:48pm

Jammin' Jimmy Bean - @Tim, it wasn't aimed at you, just setting the record straight. @ Robin, Robert Plant asks this

question during a performance of "Stairway to Heaven" on "The Song Remains the Same". I do remember, but I'm too busy trying to ENLIGHTEN folks. (^:
March 23 at 9:51pm

Tim Kirby - *Sorry Jim, I could only get through half of it. But I DID try to watch it just for you. It was an attack piece, and proves my point about Olbermann being a commentator. It was all opinion. While I agree that the name calling by members of the tea party movement are deplorable and cast a shadow over the entire movement, that stuff does happen on both sides of the aisle. Did you see my post about the threats on Ann Coulters life at a speaking engagement? I realize you do not like nor approve of Ann, but I am sure you realize that threats of violence against her do not really help your cause. Olbermann resorted to name calling to appeal to the baser instincts of his viewers the same way that Limbaugh does his listeners. They are really two sides of the same coin. I mean come on, calling Jon Voight and "evolutionary regressive" and I am supposed to take him seriously as a journalist? And why is anyone who disagrees with the President a racist? And the comment about not accepting the outcome of the election, there were eight years of listening to "Bush stole the election". And with Obama's approval ratings down around 44% I think some of the people who did vote for him are pulling away, not just those of us who did not. I am leaving the conversation on that note because I don't want things to get all heated up like they did the other night. Robin and I have just reached a point of being internet friendly and I am not going to* *push it. :-) Y'all have a nice rest of this discussion without me. I think I have given you plenty of ammo to "bash" me with. ;-)*

March 23 at 10:03pm

Rosie O'Donnell's Essay "Now You Get Mad" With Response

On March 31, Michael Tipsword posted an essay by Rosie O'Donnell on his page. I couldn't really find anywhere else to include it in the pages so here it is in its entirety, with my complete response.

"And NOW you get angry?!?!?

You didn't get mad when the Supreme Court stopped a legal recount and appointed a President.

You didn't get mad when Cheney allowed Energy company officials to dictate
energy policy.

You didn't get mad when a covert CIA operative got outed.

You didn't get mad when the Patriot Act got passed.

You didn't get mad when we illegally invaded a country that posed no threat to us.

You didn't get mad when we spent over 600 billion(and counting) on said illegal war.

You didn't get mad when over 10 billion dollars just disappeared in Iraq.

You didn't get mad when you found out we were torturing people.

You didn't get mad when the government was illegally wiretapping Americans.
You didn't get mad when we didn't catch Bin Laden.

180

You didn't get mad when you saw the horrible conditions at Walter Reed.

You didn't get mad when we let a major US city, New Orleans, drown.

You didn't get mad when we gave a 900 billion tax break to the rich.

You didn't get mad when the deficit hit the trillion dollar mark.

You finally got mad when the government decided that people in America deserved the right to see a doctor if they are sick. Yes, illegal wars, lies, corruption, torture, stealing your tax dollars to make the rich richer, are all okay with you, but helping other Americans...oh hell no."

Rosie O'Donnell via Huffington Post

Tim Kirby - *OK, point by point,*

1. The Supreme court did NOT appoint a president. He won every recount including the unofficial one conducted later, using the most liberal standards for vote counting. I am so tired of that same old argument being pulled out all time. Gore lost, it was 10 years ago, get over it.

2. Cheney was the Vice President, he was not in a position to allow anything. Look at Biden, what has he done other than put his foot in Obama's mouth over and over. The VP is not a powerful position in the government unless the president dies, think Lyndon Johnson who assassinated himself to the top.

3. Plame was a paper pusher in Virginia, not an "operative".

4. There are many parts of the Patriot Act that concerned Conservatives. However, we understand what is needed to secure the Nation in these days of global terrorism.

5. The war was voted on by Congress, meeting the requirements of the War Powers Act, therefor, legal. Same old Lib tripe from Vietnam. The Hussein Regime was a threat to the stability of the region, thereby being a threat to us. Also a major threat to Israel, who used to be a close ally until the last year.

6. I'll give you that one (other than the illegal part), war is expensive.

7. It was more like 12 million, and it didn't disappear, it was used to pay civil service employees and contractors, many of whom hadn't been paid in months. After the invasion there was not a good banking system in place.

8. Torture is subjective. We were water boarding, keeping people awake, playing loud music and making them make naked pyramids. Maybe that is torture, but

if it saved 1 American life then OK. Rosie is making it sound like we were driving bamboo under fingernails.

9. That makes it sound like everyone was having their phone conversations listened to. It is a very misleading statement and one that the left has been throwing around for almost a decade as a scare tactic. It was targeted wire taps to find people who wanted to do damage to our Country and take American lives.

10. How do you know we don't have Bin Laden. If we did, putting him on display would make him even more powerful. I don't think that we do, but it is not for lack of trying. It is not like we are getting huge amounts of cooperation from our "friends" in Pakistan, which is probably where he is hiding now.

11. Yes we did. No one was not outraged by Walter Reed, but in fairness, not all the wards were like the one that was shown on the news. They were extremely overcrowded (which also is not right), and had to use some older wards. The entire situation "made us mad".

12. We didn't LET New Orleans drown. Katrina was a hell storm. The levees didn't hold. That is what happens when you build on the coast, below sea level. And seeing New Orleans go under damn near killed me, that is my home away from home.

13. No problems at all with tax breaks for the rich. That is simple economics. When the rich have more money, they spend more money. When they spend more money, jobs are created for the not so rich. Besides, it is their money, why should the government take it? I don't

want them taking mine. This is simple another attempt at sparking class warfare. Divide and conquer. Besides, last time I checked Rosie was rich.

14. Yes we did. Any true fiscal conservative was completely "mad" about the deficit, which has grown more in the last year under Obama that it did in the last 16 years under Clinton and Bush. I was never a fan of the Bush stimulus (with the exception of tax cuts) and what it did to the economy. I am equally as unhappy with the Obama stimulus. AND, the HC bill is going to drive the deficit even higher. Just as an aside, Obama was elected in Nov., in Jan my paycheck decreased by $30 when he allowed the Bush cuts to expire. THAT is something I am mad about.

And yes, we are mad as hell about the Health Care bill. It violates the Constitution, it was passed in a way that violates the Constitution, it was passed against the will of the majority of the American people (2/3 were against) by people who are supposed to REPRESENT the will of the people. So yes, we are mad.

In closing, Rosie O'Donnell is a wackjob who is doing more to discredit the left than anyone on the right could possibly do. She thinks, and has publicly stated that the Bush administration brought down the towers on 9/11. We have one of those on the right too, Jesse Ventura, we just tend to ignore him.

March 31 at 8:51pm

Appendix A

[This is a treatise on religion that I original posted on its own in November of 2009. In the course of Lisa Hoag's health care thread it was rehashed because I wanted to be a smart ass to someone who was repeatedly calling for a religious conversation. To be fair, he was being facetious and trying to point out how divisive our conversation was becoming. I posted in this essay with the tag line "Aren't you glad you asked." I removed this from the original thread in this book because it was so far off topic and because many of my friends would prefer not to read it again. I am including it here so that there will be a sense completeness to the thread.]

Tim Kirby - *You have been asking Brian so here you go...*

I have never been able to get my head around the idea of a perfect God creating a world with so much suffering. There are evil people in the world, natural disasters, starvation, etc. I have never bought into free will explaining evil, the world could have been created perfect, with no evil and we still could have had free will, we just would have a different set of options. I also never believed that God has a reason for the kind of suffering that my mother went through. There is no reason that could make that the wish of a benevolent deity. However, there are too many things that I see that cannot be explained by a cosmic accident either, so I was not willing to write off creation altogether. Enter Gnosticism. If the universe was created by Samael/the demiurge, and he was a flawed being then it stands to reason that creation would be flawed as well. There being the reason for suffering and evil. It also explains the difference between the Gods of the Old and New Testaments. Samael in the Old and the Transcendent Perfect God in the New. But Gnosticism still left me searching for answers because of my Christian upbringing. If the only way to salvation was through Gnosis, and only the spiritually mature could attain Gnosis, then what about the rest of us? The secret teachings of Jesus were only given to a few who were deemed ready and we were told that the rest were not ready to hear and would not understand. But I was raised to believe that all had a chance at salvation. After lots of study and thought it hit me. It just came to my mind and everything was clear and all the pieces popped into place. Jesus of Nazareth was more than just the son of God; he was the son on Sophia/Wisdom. He brought the knowledge of the transcendent God to everyone because before him only a very few even strived for Gnosis and most believed Samael was the true god. So Jesus WAS Gnosis. We were told as much when he said "I am the way, the truth and the light". He was Gnosis for the masses allowing all to have salvation.

This all comes from scripture. Either from the canonical Bible or from the Nag Hamidi scrolls. There were a lot of Christian texts in circulation before Council of Nicaea selected those that would make up the canon. As an example, In the Apocryphon of John: Part II of the Gospel of John also called the Secret Book of John it states "This gloomy ruler has three names: The first is Yaldaboath, the second is Sakla, the third is Samael. He is wicked in his mindlessness that is in him. He said I am god and there is no other god but me, since he did not know where his own strength had come from." Meaning he was unaware that his power had come from the One.

This is an attempt to understand all evil and suffering in creation. That is the basis of Gnosticism as I see it, the search for knowledge. Gnosis translates to "knowledge". I cannot accept a benevolent deity who allows the kind of evil that has someone murdered in their sleep. OK, the murderer had free will what about the victim? This was always glossed over in my Sunday school classes with "The Lord has a plan." I have discussed these questions with Protestant Ministers and Catholic Priests and no one has ever given a satisfactory answer.

Ponder on this, the Cathars and Albigensians were growing in numbers and popularity until Pope Innocent III declared them Heretics and had them massacred.

Rev. Dr. Tim Kirby